Syria

Syria

BY NEL YOMTOV

Enchantment of the World™
Second Series

CHILDREN'S PRESS®

An Imprint of Scholastic Inc.

New York   Toronto   London   Auckland   Sydney
Mexico City   New Delhi   Hong Kong
Danbury, Connecticut

Frontispiece: **Umayyad Mosque, Damascus**

Consultant: Steve Tamari, Assistant Professor, Department of Historical Studies, Southern Illinois University Edwardsville, Edwardsville, Illinois

Please note: All statistics are as up-to-date as possible at the time of publication.

Book production by The Design Lab

Library of Congress Cataloging-in-Publication Data
Yomtov, Nelson.
  Syria / Nel Yomtov.
      pages cm.—(Enchantment of the world. Second series)
  Includes bibliographical references and index.
  ISBN 978-0-531-23679-6 (lib. bdg.)
1. Syria—Juvenile literature. I. Title.
  DS93.Y66 2013
  956.91—dc23   2013000088

1 2 3 4 5 6 7 8 9 10 R 23 22 21 20 19 18 17 16 15 14

Children near Hamah

Contents

CHAPTER 1   Ancient and Modern **8**

CHAPTER 2   From Mountain to Desert **14**

CHAPTER 3   The Natural World **26**

CHAPTER 4   Crossroads in the Middle East **34**

CHAPTER 5   A Powerful Government **56**

CHAPTER 6   A Diverse Economy **68**

CHAPTER 7   People and Language **78**

CHAPTER 8   Religious Life **90**

CHAPTER 9   Rich Traditions **102**

CHAPTER 10   Family, Food, and Fun **116**

Timeline **128**

Fast Facts **130**

To Find Out More **134**

Index **136**

Left to right: **Almond trees, gazelle, clay tablet with cuneiform, snow in Damascus, Palmyra**

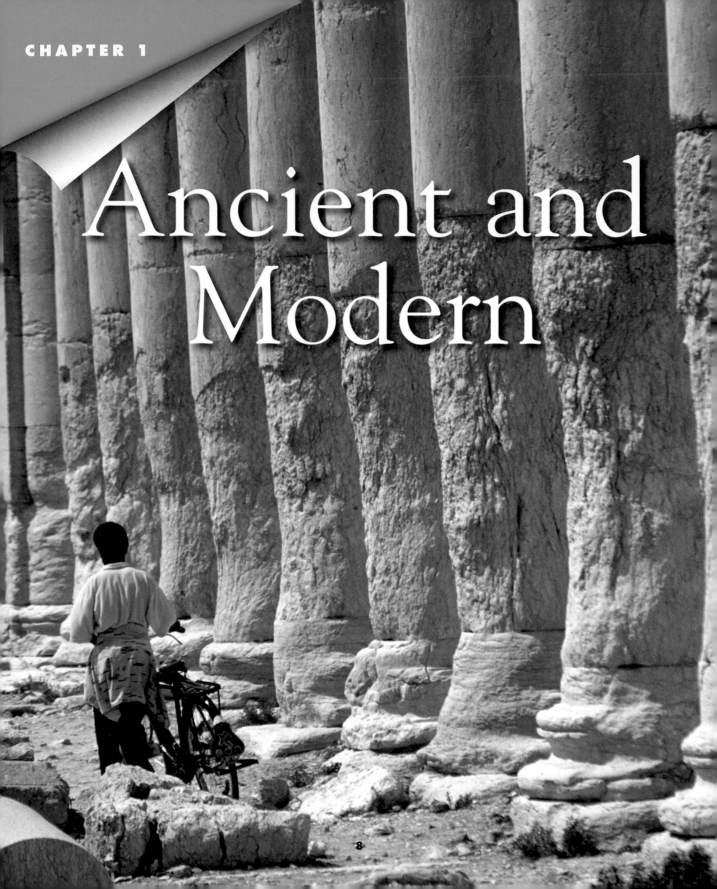

CHAPTER 1

Ancient and Modern

IT IS OFTEN SAID THAT IN SYRIA, THE PAST IS ALWAYS present. Syria is located on the eastern shores of the Mediterranean Sea, in a region where Europe, Asia, and Africa meet. Because of its location, it has played a critical role in world history for thousands of years. It has been home to many great thinkers and religious leaders. Complex civilizations sprouted along the banks of the nearby Tigris and Euphrates Rivers.

For thousands of years, Syria was both a destination for migrating peoples and a battleground for competing empires. With its fertile lands, developed trade routes, and intellectual accomplishments, many different cultures invaded, occupied, and colonized Syria. Many peoples, including the Egyptians, Babylonians, Romans, Arabs, European Christian crusaders, French, and British, have left an enduring mark on the landscape and culture of Syria.

Opposite: **A man walks through the ruins of Palmyra, which was a major city on the east-west trade route through the Syrian Desert two thousand years ago.**

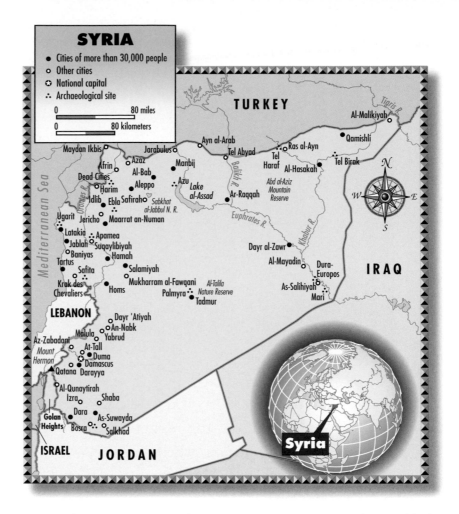

In Palmyra, in central Syria, visitors can see the reddish-brown ruins of ancient Greek, Roman, and Byzantine temples standing solemnly on the desert floor. In Bosra, in the south, a well-preserved Roman amphitheater sits alongside ancient Christian churches and one of the world's oldest surviving mosques, Muslim houses of worship. Throughout the country, huge castles and fortresses built a thousand years ago still stand. They were erected during the Crusades, when Europeans were trying to seize control of holy lands from Muslims. Today, Syria abounds with countless monuments and reminders of its long, rich history.

Syria is much more than a land of ancient ruins and religious sites. Today, networks of modern highways and railroad systems stretch over ancient battlefields. Huge hydroelectric dams control the flow of the Euphrates and Orontes Rivers and provide electricity to bustling towns and cities. High-rise office buildings and apartments, universities, sports arenas, and modern airports are common in the capital of Damascus and other large cities.

Struggles of an Independent Nation

Despite its five-thousand-year history, Syria only became independent in 1946. In the decades since, it has experienced much political instability. One military takeover after another rocked

Cars often clog the streets of Damascus, so many people travel around the city by minibus instead.

the nation. In 1970, Minister of Defense Hafez al-Assad gained power in a bloodless military coup. Al-Assad served as Syria's president from 1971 until his death in 2000. Throughout his rule, al-Assad controlled Syria's government and economy tightly. The Syrian people had few political rights. People who spoke out against the government were punished harshly.

Hafez's son Bashar al-Assad assumed power in 2000. Bashar promised many reforms. Under his leadership, Syria's government eased some restrictions on speech and the press. But nearly all of Syria's radio and television stations remain owned by the state. Al-Assad's ruling Baath Party controls almost all the newspapers. Most Syrians believe that not enough has been done to promote more democratic policies.

President Bashar al-Assad (center) stands with military leaders at a ceremony in 2011. He was thirty-four years old when he succeeded his father as president.

Protest and Uncertainty

Al-Assad's rule was shaken in 2011 when a string of peaceful protests calling for political freedom led to a brutal government crackdown by the Syrian army. By the end of 2012, Syria was in the grip of a civil war. Tens of thousands of protesters, armed rebels, and Syrian forces had been killed.

The Syrian people face an uncertain future. Only when the violence ends will they be able to tackle their nation's many other challenges: a sagging economy that has been damaged by the civil war, government censorship and corruption, and high levels of unemployment. Until that time, Syrians try to maintain life as usual—praying at mosques and churches, visiting friends and family, working, and hoping for a better tomorrow.

Residents of Damascus carry the coffin of a man killed in Syria's civil war in 2012. They wave Syrian independence flags, the national flag when Syria first became independent. This flag has become the symbol of opposition to the al-Assad regime.

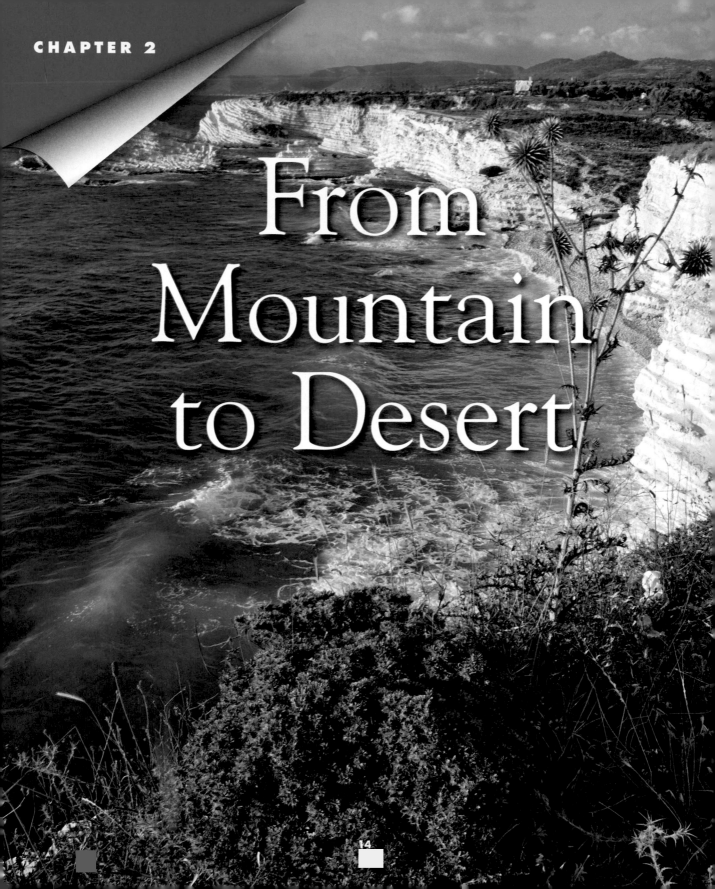

CHAPTER 2

From Mountain to Desert

SYRIA LIES IN THE CENTER OF THE MIDDLE EAST, the part of the world where the continents of Europe, Asia, and Africa meet. It shares its borders with Turkey to the north, Iraq to the east and southeast, Jordan to the south, and Israel, Lebanon, and the Mediterranean Sea to the west.

The nation covers 71,498 square miles (185,180 square kilometers), making it roughly the same size as the state of North Dakota. About 500 square miles (1,300 sq km) of its land, a region called the Golan Heights, has been occupied by Israel since the Six-Day War of 1967.

Syria has four major natural land formations: a coastal plain; mountain ranges that run from north to south and separate the coastal plain from the interior; a fertile plain east of the mountains; and the Syrian Desert.

Opposite: **Limestone cliffs line the coast near Latakia. Syria has about 120 miles (200 km) of coastline along the Mediterranean Sea.**

Coastal Plain

In northern Syria, the Mediterranean coastline is marked by rugged, rocky cliffs. Moving southward, the coastline eases into sandy beaches that stretch for miles. This region receives

Syria's Geographic Features

Area: 71,498 square miles (185,180 sq km)

Highest Elevation: Mount Hermon (below), 9,232 feet (2,814 m) above sea level

Lowest Elevation: Near the Sea of Galilee, in an area occupied by Israel, 656 feet (200 m) below sea level

Longest River: Euphrates River (right); 420 miles (680 km) flows through Syria

Largest Lake: Lake al-Jabbul, 60 square miles (155 sq km)

Largest City (2010 est.): Aleppo, population 2,900,000

Highest Recorded Temperature: 121°F (50°C), at Al-Hasakah, July 30, 2000

Lowest Recorded Temperature: –9.4°F (–23°C), at Idlib, January 16, 1950

Average High Temperature: In Damascus, 55°F (13°C) in January, 98°F (37°C) in July; in Latakia, 60°F (16°C) in January, 84°F (29°C) in July

Average Annual Rainfall: Coastal areas and western mountains: 29 to 39 inches (75 to 100 cm); inland: 4 to 10 inches (10 to 25 cm)

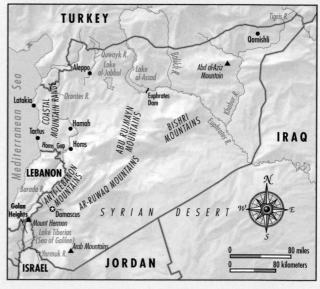

about 35 inches (89 centimeters) of rainfall each year. Much of Syria's greenest and most fertile land lies near the coast, making it home to a bustling agricultural community that produces most of the country's vegetables and fruits. Orange, lemon, apple, cherry, and peach trees grow in orchards.

Mountain Ranges

Most of Syria's mountains are located in the west and south. The Coastal Mountain Range forms the main barrier between the coastline and the interior. These mountains rise to about 5,000 feet (1,500 meters) at the northern end of the range. South of the Coastal Mountain Range is a narrow corridor called the Homs Gap, which allows easy passage from the coast to Syria's interior. The Homs Gap has been a pathway for traders and invading armies for centuries. Today, one of Syria's main oil pipelines runs from the desert through the Homs Gap to the port city of Tartus. A highway and railroad also cut through the Homs Gap. The rail line connects the city of Homs with the Lebanese port of Tripoli.

While the western side of the Coastal Mountain Range receives significant rainfall from the Mediterranean, little rain falls on the eastern side of the mountains. There, scrubby grasslands provide good grazing grounds for sheep and goats.

South of the Homs Gap lie the Anti-Lebanon Mountains, which mark Syria's border with Lebanon. Mount Hermon, rising to 9,232 feet (2,814 m), lies in the southern reaches of this mountain chain. It is Syria's highest point. The Anti-Lebanon Mountains gradually decrease in height until they reach the

The land in northern Syria is generally flat and fertile.

Golan Heights, Syrian territory occupied by Israel. The south-eastern slopes of Mount Hermon are also occupied by Israel.

The now-extinct volcanic peaks of the Arab Mountains, once called the Druze Mountains, lie in the southwest. Many Syrians who follow the Druze religion live in this rocky region that is marked by caves and lava flows. The Abu Rujmayn and the Bishri Mountains lie in Syria's vast desert.

Fertile Plain

East of the Coastal Mountain Range and Anti-Lebanon Mountains is a vast grassy plain called a steppe. The steppe stretches from Jordan in the south to Turkey in the north. It then turns east along the Turkish border. The steppe has an average altitude of 2,000 feet (600 m). The climate is generally windy and cold. In winter, snow often covers the ground.

This treeless plain receives up to 20 inches (50 cm) of rainfall annually, which is enough to grow grain. Syria's irrigation systems, which carry water from rivers and streams to the fields of the plain, make the plain's soil particularly fertile.

Floodwaters from the many rivers that flow through or along the steppe, including the Euphrates, Orontes, Barada, and Yarmuk, further enrich the soil of the region. Farmers on the steppe provide much of the food and livestock consumed by Syrians. Temperatures on the steppe can top 99 degrees Fahrenheit (37 degrees Celsius) in the summer and reach as low as 34°F (1°C) in the winter.

A thousand years ago in the city of Hamah, Syrians built giant waterwheels called *norias* to lift water from the Orontes River into artificial channels. The water was used to irrigate fields.

Desert

The Syrian Desert covers more than half of Syria and extends into Iraq and Jordan. The desert makes up most of Syria's southeastern territory. It was formed by lava flows from the Arab Mountains. The western portion of the desert is hard and rocky, while the eastern part is sandy. The desert has extremely hot, dry summers and cold winters. Temperatures can climb as high as 114°F (46°C) in the summer. The annual rainfall is usually no more than 5 inches (13 cm).

Within the desert are a few places of greenery, called oases. Rivers, underground springs, and wells feed the trees and short grasses found in an oasis. The only human inhabitants of the

Date palm trees thrive in the Palmyra oasis.

Syrian Desert are the nomadic Bedouin people. The Bedouin often set up tents around the oases and graze their sheep, horses, and camels there. Then they pack up their belongings and set off into the desert in search of more water and grazing.

Rivers and Lakes

Syria's most important rivers are the Euphrates and the Orontes. The Euphrates flows a total of 2,235 miles (3,597 kilometers), and roughly 420 miles (680 km) of it is in Syria. The river begins in Turkey, flows south into Syria, and then exits into Iraq, where it empties into the Persian Gulf. As the Euphrates snakes its way through Syria, it is fed by the Balikh and the Khabur Rivers. Together, their waters nourish the rich farmland of the Syrian plateau.

Since 1973, Syria has built three dams on the Euphrates. The dams provide water to irrigate vast tracts of land. They also produce hydroelectricity that helps power the nation. The Tabqa Dam is Syria's largest dam. Lake al-Assad, a reservoir 50 miles (80 km) long, was created as a result of the dam's construction.

The Orontes River flows for 250 miles (400 km), beginning in Lebanon and entering Syria south of Homs. It then flows into Turkey and empties into the Mediterranean Sea. Dams on the Orontes River at Homs and Hamah irrigate western Syria to make the region agriculturally productive. The dams also provide hydroelectricity to local industry and businesses.

Lake al-Assad is used to irrigate farmland and is an important source of drinking water for the city of Aleppo.

The Barada River begins in the Anti-Lebanon Mountains, flows to Damascus and then northeastward into the desert. The Barada feeds al-Ghutah Oasis, the fertile area where Damascus stands. Throughout history, people have diverted the life-giving waters of the river to irrigate the lands around Damascus. Without these efforts, Damascus would have been an arid outpost rather than the thriving metropolis it has been for thousands of years.

Lake al-Jabbul, located southeast of Aleppo, is Syria's largest natural lake. It covers an area of roughly 60 square miles (155 sq km). The region around the lake is used mainly for tourism, livestock grazing, and salt mining.

Climate

Syria's climate varies widely from west to east. The western coastal plains along the Mediterranean are hot and humid. In summer, temperatures can soar as high as 99°F (37°C). Winter temperatures along the coast usually range between 49°F (9°C) and 68°F (20°C).

Moving eastward, the Coastal Mountain Range and Anti-Lebanon Mountains block winds that carry in moisture from the Mediterranean. The western slopes, therefore, are wetter and cooler than the eastern slopes and interior land. The mountains experience average temperatures of 72°F (22°C) in summer and 42°F (6°C) in winter. The plateau has hot summers and cool winters. Temperatures can reach 104°F (40°C) in the summer and drop to less than 45°F (7°C) in the winter.

Syria's rainy season is during the winter, with the most rain falling on the coast and the nearby mountains. Annual

A Deadly Earthquake

Syria has a long history of destructive earthquakes. Several of the nation's most heavily populated cities, including Damascus, Aleppo, Homs, and Hamah, sit atop the Dead Sea Fault System. The system is responsible for frequent earthquake rumblings in the region. One of the most destructive earthquakes in history struck Aleppo in October 1138. It is estimated that 230,000 people were killed in the disaster. A cru-sader castle in nearby Harim was destroyed, and the Muslim-occupied fort of al-Atarib collapsed, killing 600 guardsmen. Several smaller towns and forts crumbled. In Aleppo, the walls of the Citadel collapsed, killing hundreds. Many homes were destroyed. Fortunately, many residents of the city fled to the countryside when they felt the first shocks. The Aleppo earthquake is thought to be the fourth-deadliest earthquake in history.

precipitation, including snow in the higher elevations, varies from 20 to 40 inches (51 to 102 cm) and can top 50 inches (127 cm) in some regions.

The Syrian Desert receives little rainfall, usually no more than 5 inches (13 cm) annually. In some years, it may not receive any rain at all. The land is arid and plant life is very sparse.

Children play in the snow in Damascus. It snows an average of two days a year in the city.

Looking at Syria's Cities

With an estimated population of 2,900,000 people, Aleppo (below) is Syria's largest city. Located in the northwest, Aleppo has been inhabited since about 5000 BCE, making it one of the world's oldest cities. In ancient times, Aleppo served as a major trading point between the Mediterranean Sea and the many civilizations that flourished in Mesopotamia, the fertile region between the Tigris and Euphrates Rivers, most of which is now in Iraq. About 74 percent of Aleppo's residents are Sunni Muslims. The city is also home to one of the largest Christian populations in the Middle East. Textile manufacturing, chemical production, and tourism are among Aleppo's leading industries. Visitors seek out such landmarks as the Citadel, an enormous fortress built about 3,500 years ago.

The capital of Damascus is Syria's second-largest city, with a population of about 2,500,000. The nation's third-largest city is Homs, with a population of roughly

1,300,000. Homs is located on the Orontes River in western Syria. The earliest settlements in Homs date back to about 2300 BCE. Throughout the centuries, Homs has been an important agricultural market and trading center. It serves as an important link between Syria's inland cities and the Mediterranean coast. The Mosque of Khalid ibn al-Walid is one of the city's key landmarks. It contains the tomb of ibn al-Walid, an Arab general who led the Muslim conquest of Syria in the 630s.

Latakia (above), Syria's fourth-largest city, is home to roughly 991,000 people. It is located in northwestern Syria on the Mediterranean. Latakia is the country's largest port, and also a manufacturing center. People have inhabited the area for about 3,500 years, although the current city was founded in the third century BCE under the Greek Seleucid Empire. Latakia's beaches are popular tourist destinations, where people enjoy windsurfing and other water sports.

Syria's fifth-largest city, Hamah, is located on the Orontes River in west-central Syria. Hamah is home to roughly 854,000 residents. People have inhabited the site for at least 3,000 years. Hamah's most notable landmarks are seventeen *norias*, huge wooden waterwheels that were once part of the region's irrigation system. The norias, which today are mostly unused, date back to the twelfth century.

CHAPTER 3

The Natural World

DESERTS COVER MORE THAN HALF OF SYRIA. THESE regions are so hot and dry that few plants and animals can survive there. Even in the more temperate mountains and steppe, wild animal life is sparse.

Opposite: **Forests cover the mountainsides near the Fortress of Saladin in western Syria.**

Plant Life

Forests cover only a small portion of Syria's total area. They are found mainly in the mountains, especially in the Coastal Mountain Range. Firs, pines, and cedars grow in the north on the rainy western side of the range. On the eastern side of the mountains and farther south, heartier plants that do not require much water abound. These include myrtle, boxwood, arbutus, and wild olive.

Some forest plants are used for commercial purposes. These include wild pistachio, an important oil-rich fruit. Other commercially important forest plants include sumac, which is used as a spice; laurel, which is used in making cosmetics; and licorice, which is used in some medicines.

Many trees in Syria have been cut down for their wood, turning forests into areas of scrub underbrush, where plants such as garigue and maquis grow. Syria has begun a reforestation project in the mountains north of Latakia, and the government now protects some forests.

Lemon trees and orange trees are found along the western coast. The steppe supports no tree life other than an occasional hawthorn tree. People have planted all other trees in the region, such as those growing in orchards in Damascus and Aleppo and along the banks of the Euphrates and Orontes Rivers.

During spring, jasmine, orange blossoms, and bougainvillea flourish, adding splashes of color and sweet scents to the land. By summer, however, the extreme heat causes them to wither and die.

An almond orchard near Homs. Almond trees produce abundant pink or white blossoms in the spring.

Animal Life

Syria was once home to thriving populations of wolves, boars, deer, hyenas, bears, and many kinds of birds. In ancient Syria, people mainly survived by hunting wild animals. Elephants, lions, and wild bulls lived on the Syrian steppe. Some civilizations hunted them for sport. These animals, however, were hunted nearly to extinction by the early 1900s.

Today, Syria has about 130 kinds of mammals. The Syrian brown bear is the nation's largest animal. Small populations of deer, foxes, wild pigs, and hyenas still roam the remote areas of the country. Animal life in the desert includes gazelles and jerboas, long-legged rodents that hop like kangaroos across the sands. Moles and shrews also inhabit the desert. Bats make up about 20 percent of all mammal life in Syria. Various lizards, vipers, and chameleons also make their homes in the sunbaked desert regions.

The camel is an important domesticated animal in Syria. For centuries, camels were the main form of transportation for Bedouin nomads. Although many modern Bedouin use trucks

The Syrian Hamster

The Syrian hamster, also known as the golden hamster, is a small rodent native to Syria. Adult Syrian hamsters grow to lengths of between 5 and 7 inches (13 and 18 cm). Wild hamsters sleep during the day deep in burrows and wake in the evening to search for food. They feed mainly on grains, seeds, and nuts. Syrian hamsters are one of the most common types of hamsters kept as pets. They are popular because they are small, meek, and curious.

or jeeps to travel across the desert, some still use camels. Domesticated mules are frequently used to carry supplies in the mountains. Other domesticated animals common in Syria include horses, donkeys, sheep, goats, and chickens.

About 399 species of birds live in or pass through Syria. Aquatic birds such as flamingos, pelicans, geese, and ducks feed and nest near water. Eagles, falcons, owls, and buzzards make their nests in mountain cliffs. The steppe eagle lives on the Syrian steppe, feeding on small rodents and mammals.

About 70 species of freshwater fish swim in Syrian waters. They include mullet, tilapia, carp, catfish, eel, and mosquito fish. The Syrian government operates many fish farms, where fish are bred for use as food for the Syrian people.

Environmental Concerns

Syria faces many environmental problems. From the congested streets of large cities, such as Damascus and Aleppo, to the barren, arid deserts, Syria's environment is in a fragile state. The lack of clean water is one of the country's most serious issues.

Little rain falls in large parts of Syria. Meanwhile, industry and construction pollute much of the water supply. Additionally, a great deal of Syria's water is needed for agriculture, and industrial waste polluting that water risks the health of the nation.

Air pollution is a serious problem in many urban areas. Heavy industrialization and old motor vehicles that emit dangerous chemicals into the air are the main causes of smog and pollution. This pollution is dangerous to human health. It also harms the plant life in cities.

Pelicans are one of the many waterbirds found in Syria. They have large throat pouches, which they use to scoop up fish.

Only about one-third of the land in Syria is suitable for farming. Overgrazing and outdated farming techniques have stripped some areas of all their vegetation. Without plant life to hold the fertile topsoil in place, it blows or washes away with the wind and rain. Parts of the once-fertile steppe have become desert, so there is even less land available to grow crops.

To combat these environmental problems, the Syrian government adopted the National Environmental Action Plan (NEAP) in 2003. NEAP's goal was to develop programs

Pollution clouds the air in Aleppo.

Wildlife Reserves

In 1991, Syria established al-Talila Nature Reserve, the nation's first wildlife reserve. The reserve is home to a wide variety of mammals, plants, insects, birds, and reptiles. Ibis birds, thought to be extinct, were discovered at al-Talila. Several different species of insects that had not been found anywhere in the world were also found at the reserve, including a species of ladybug called al-Talila.

Syria also has more than twenty other reserves. These include al-Thawra Reserve, which is located on an island in Lake al-Assad in north-central Syria. The island is only 1.25 miles (2 km) long and 32 feet (10 m) wide, but it is home to a variety of wildlife, including foxes, deer, hawks, pigeons, gulls, and partridges. Several years ago, al-Thawra was a breeding ground for gazelles (left), which were close to becoming extinct in Syria. Since that time, the gazelles have been released into the wild. Numerous plants, including oleas and eucalypti, also live in al-Thawra Reserve.

that would prevent misuse of land and water resources, reduce the effects of pollution, and protect natural resources. The government built sewage and waste management plants in several cities. It also began an aggressive tree-planting program between the desert and the steppe. This was intended to replenish the soil and prevent the desert from expanding. More than six hundred trees were also planted around Damascus, and plans were adopted to clean up several waterways. A lack of government funding to carry out Syria's green programs has prevented large-scale environmental improvements from being made nationwide.

CHAPTER 4

Crossroads in the Middle East

THE ANCIENT AREA KNOWN AS GREATER SYRIA WAS much larger than present-day Syria. Greater Syria included the land that became Lebanon, Jordan, Israel, and parts of Turkey and Iraq. This ancient territory was a crossroads of three continents—trekked across by traders, invading armies, and wandering nomads.

Opposite: **Ancient clay tablets covered with a form of writing called cuneiform have been found in several sites in Syria.**

Early Civilizations

Evidence indicates that humans have been living in Syria for about 150,000 years. Human remains, tools, and weapons from that time have been unearthed at Mari on the Euphrates River and near Latakia on the Mediterranean coast.

Early settlements along the Euphrates date back to around 9000 BCE. The world's oldest wall painting, now on display at a museum in Aleppo, was found in the region at Djade-al-Mughara in 2007.

The Palace of Ebla dates to about 2400 BCE. The Akkadians destroyed the city in the 2200s BCE.

In about 4000 BCE, a large city began to develop in northeast Syria, near present-day Tel Birak. The city was located in an area between the Tigris and Euphrates Rivers, an area called Mesopotamia. Tel Birak grew to become a major city but collapsed in about 1000 BCE. The people of Tel Birak traded extensively with people in the nearby city of Ebla.

Ebla was a major commercial center, located about 40 miles (65 km) south of present-day Aleppo. The city was founded in about 3500 BCE. The Ebla kingdom was the most powerful in northern Syria. Its territory at one time included northern Syria, Iran, Anatolia (part of what is now Turkey), and southern Mesopotamia. More than seventeen thousand clay tablets with cuneiform writing dating to about 2400 BCE were discovered at the site. Cuneiform writing features wedge-shaped characters made with a pointed writing tool. Each character is a word. The tablets indicate that Ebla traded with Egypt and Mesopotamia.

At the same time as Ebla thrived, other important cities were also established in Syria. Between roughly 3500 BCE and 1800 BCE, Damascus, Aleppo, and Mari were founded.

The city of Ugarit flourished on Syria's northwest coast. Ugarit was an important port and the starting point for the trade route into Mesopotamia. The Phoenicians, a seafaring people whose civilization was based in what is now Lebanon, left many clay tablets in Ugarit. These tablets are especially important because the symbols that appear on them provide the basis for the alphabet used in most countries today. The thirty different symbols found on the tablets were easier to read and write than cuneiform.

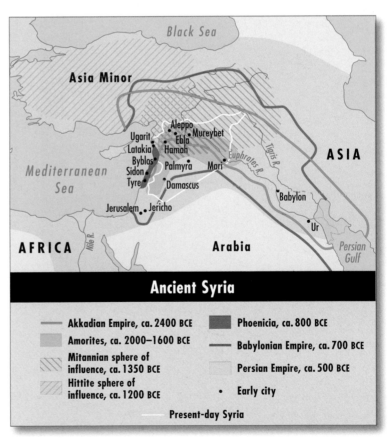

Invaders and Settlers

The location of Greater Syria made it a target for invading armies. In about 2400 BCE, the

Amorites, a people with lands west of Mesopotamia, gained control of northern Syria. They made Aleppo the center of their kingdom. In about 2250 BCE, King Naram-Sin of Akkad, a kingdom in southern Mesopotamia, crushed the armies of Ebla and destroyed the city.

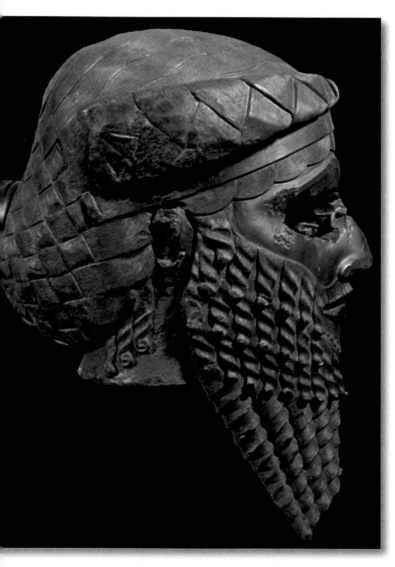

A bronze head of the Akkadian king Naram-Sin

The Amorites fell when Egypt invaded Greater Syria, taking control of the south. The Hittites, from present-day Turkey, controlled the north. Large numbers of people from foreign lands continued to migrate into Syria. Hebrews moved into the north from present-day Israel. Aramaeans, from present-day Saudi Arabia, settled in northern and central Syria.

Babylonians, Assyrians, and Persians

Different powers continued to vie for control of Greater Syria. The Babylonian kingdom was located between the Tigris and Euphrates Rivers in Mesopotamia, in what is now Iraq. In the eighteenth century BCE, Hammurabi, the king of Babylon, extended his empire's reach into Syria. In 732 BCE, the

The Ruins at Palmyra

In a desert oasis northeast of Damascus are the ruins of the ancient city of Palmyra. Founded around 1500 BCE, Palmyra became a major trading link between eastern countries such as Persia, India, and China, and western countries in Europe. The city reached the peak of its importance during the first and second centuries CE. The Romans destroyed Palmyra in 273 CE, and the city never regained its earlier glory.

Today, ancient Palmyra is a maze of reddish lime-stone ruins. The most impressive building on the site is the huge Temple of Baal, which was originally a Greek temple. Visitors can also see ruins of a Roman theater, tombs, government buildings, baths, and dozens of columns. And more ruins are still being unearthed. In 2008, a 1,200-year-old church was uncovered. It is the largest church ever found in Syria.

Assyrians conquered Damascus. Their rule, however, was short-lived, and the Babylonians retook Syria.

In 539 BCE, Cyrus the Great of Persia, present-day Iran, defeated the Babylonians. Cyrus made Syria part of the Persian Empire, which was at the time the largest empire the world had ever seen. It ranged from northern Africa in the west to what is now Pakistan in the east, and from the Black Sea in the north to the Arabian Sea in the south. The empire was efficiently governed. As long as the king's subjects paid their taxes, he did not interfere with local customs or trade. The Persians built roads that connected the empire's most important cities, established a system of gold and silver coins, and adopted Aramaic as their official language.

Apamea was an important city during the Seleucid dynasty. It was abandoned in the 1200s.

Greek, Roman, and Byzantine Control

In 332 BCE, Alexander the Great of Greece conquered the Persian Empire. Alexander left control of Syria to one of his generals, Seleucus. For more than two hundred years, Seleucus and his descendants, the Seleucids, ruled Syria. Under their administration, the Greek language and Greek thinking in science, law, and philosophy spread throughout Greater Syria. Trade expanded into Europe, India, and China.

But by the 100s BCE, the Seleucid dynasty had become weak and poorly governed. In 64 BCE, the Romans, under general Pompey, conquered the region and made Syria a Roman province. Under Roman rule, Syria prospered. New roads were built, which increased the flow of trade into and out of Syria. The Romans built aqueducts to carry water to cities and constructed irrigation networks to bring water to the fields.

During Roman rule, Christianity was born in the region that is now Israel and the Palestinian Territories. The new religion spread quickly to Syria and many parts of the vast Roman Empire. In 313 CE, the Roman emperor Constantine declared Christianity to be the entire empire's official religion. Many churches were built in Syria. Christianity soon replaced the many religions once practiced by Syrians.

Bosra, in southern Syria, was the capital of the Roman province of Arabia. The Romans built a huge theater there, which still stands.

The Warrior Queen

The actions of few men in the ancient world could match the brave deeds of the woman who ruled part of Syria in the third century CE. Queen Zenobia (ca. 240–ca. 274 CE) was born and raised in Palmyra. By 258 CE, Zenobia married the king of Palmyra. When he was assassinated in 267, Zenobia took the throne. She quickly set out to conquer new territories in memory of her husband. In 269, her army conquered Egypt and then beat back a strong counterattack by the Egyptians. She declared herself the queen of Egypt and earned the nickname Warrior Queen for her superior fighting abilities and horse-riding skills.

Leading her armies, Zenobia then conquered regions in present-day Turkey, Syria, Palestine, and Lebanon. Her victories in these regions took important trade routes away from the Romans, angering the Roman emperor Aurelian. In 273, Roman forces arrived in Syria, destroyed Palmyra, and defeated Zenobia's army. Aurelian's forces captured Zenobia and brought her to Rome as a prisoner.

Some accounts of her final fate claim she died soon after arriving in Rome, either from illness or by being beheaded. Other accounts say Aurelian spared her life and allowed her to live in a luxurious villa where she married a Roman senator and had several children.

In 330, Constantine moved the capital of the Roman Empire from Rome to Constantinople in Byzantium, present-day Turkey. The Roman Empire soon split into two parts. The Western Roman Empire was governed from Rome. The Eastern Roman Empire, called the Byzantine Empire, was governed from Constantinople.

Arab Rule

The origins of the religion of Islam date back to the seventh century CE in the Arabian Peninsula, south of Greater Syria. According to Muslim belief, in the city of Mecca in what is now Saudi Arabia, a prophet named Muhammad received messages from God. The messages form the foundation of Islam. After Muhammad's death in 632, his followers spread the word of Islam beyond the Arabian Peninsula. Khalid ibn al-Walid, a follower of Muhammad, led an invasion of Syria in 634 and took control of Damascus by 635. His victory at the Battle of Yarmuk in 636 ended 700 years of Roman rule in Syria, including 250 years of Byzantine rule.

Muawiyah I, a member of the Umayyad family, became the governor of Syria in 639. In 661, Muawiyah's followers elected him caliph, or leader, of all Muslims. He chose Damascus as the capital of the newly founded Umayyad dynasty. Muawiyah and other Umayyad caliphs expanded their rule so that they eventually controlled lands from Spain to central Asia. Under the Umayyads, Arabic became the spoken language in Syria.

The Dead Cities

The Dead Cities are a group of six hundred settlements near Aleppo that were abandoned between the eighth and the tenth centuries. Some of the settlements date back to the first century CE. They include ancient homes, temples, churches, and bathhouses. Many of the Dead Cities are well preserved and provide visitors with a fascinating look at the development of early Christianity in the region.

Muawiyah I (center) served as caliph from 661 until his death in 680. He unified the Muslim empire.

In the early 700s, the Umayyad dynasty weakened, and by 750 the Abbasid dynasty had seized control of the Muslim world. The Abbasids moved the capital to Baghdad, the present-day capital of Iraq. They promoted medicine, philosophy, science, and mathematics. They also made important technological discoveries such as the windmill and water mill. They also learned how to harness the power of nature by building dams and using wind and steam power for industry.

By the mid-900s, Abbasid control weakened. By this time, Syria had already broken up into several smaller states. Muslim Turkish armies invaded the region and conquered Syria. They set up two provinces with capitals at Damascus and Aleppo.

The European Crusaders

As the Muslim Turks continued their conquests, Western Christians began to push back against the spread of Islam. In 1096, Christian soldiers began the Crusades, a series of wars to take control of Palestine, or the Holy Land, a Middle Eastern land sacred to Christians, Jews, and Muslims. The crusaders easily won the First Crusade. They built several castles, including the Krak des Chevaliers in the Homs Gap. The crusaders conquered Turkish territory and set up outposts in Jerusalem in Palestine, Antioch in present-day Turkey, and Tripoli in present-day Libya. Several Syrian cities remained under Turkish control.

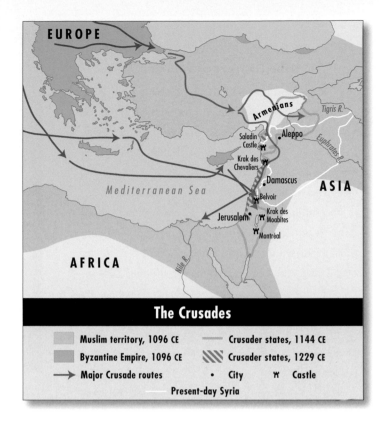

During the Third Crusade (1189–1192), Saladin, the sultan of Egypt and Syria and founder of the Ayyubid dynasty, brought the armies of several Muslim nobles under his control. In 1187, Saladin led his well-organized armies against the crusaders and pushed them out of Jerusalem, a holy city to Muslims, Christians, and Jews. At the end of the Third Crusade, Muslims and Christians agreed to a truce. The agreement guaranteed Christians safe passage to Jerusalem.

Mamluks, Mongols, and Ottomans

In 1250, the Mamluk dynasty, based in Egypt, took control from the Ayyubids. Syria prospered under the Mamluks, and Damascus became a center of trade and culture. But in 1401, people from central Asia under the leadership of a conqueror

The Fortress of Saladin

High in the Coastal Mountain Range amid a thick forest lies the Fortress of Saladin. It sits atop a long ridge between two deep ravines, narrow passages with steep, rocky sides. The castle was built primarily by European crusaders, but its long history includes the influences of many cultures.

The earliest use of the site as a fortification dates back to the first century BCE. For centuries, invading armies used the site. In 975, the Byzantines took control of the fort and began constructing stronger fortifications. European crusaders controlled the fort in the early twelfth century and built much of what stands today. Then, in 1188, Arab forces led by Saladin laid siege to the fortress. They stormed the castle and gained control of it.

Today, visitors can see the different architectural styles of the Byzantines and the crusaders. Three slender towers in the eastern wall were originally Byzantine. The towers were strengthened in the twelfth century. Towers in the southern portion of the fort were built with large stone blocks in a style typical of the crusaders.

Over the years, numerous houses of worship were constructed on the site. A crusader church and two Byzantine chapels are located in the fort's courtyards. The Arab additions to the fortress include a mosque built in the thirteenth century, a palace, and royal baths. The palace entrance is a magnificent carved gateway.

named Timur sacked Damascus and Aleppo. The attacks severely weakened the Mamluks.

In 1516, the Ottoman Turks invaded Syria and defeated the Mamluks in Aleppo. Syria became part of the new empire that the Ottomans had established. During Ottoman rule, Damascus grew in population. But over time, trade in Syria decreased, and Damascus lost some of its importance. By the beginning of the nineteenth century, the Ottoman Empire was in decline, and Syria was about to face foreign intervention once again.

Western Influence

As the Ottoman Empire faltered, the empires of Austria-Hungary and Russia grew along its northern border. The Ottomans asked France and Great Britain for help in combating these new threats. Both countries gave the Ottomans money, weapons, and military training. France became particularly influential. The French built railroads in Syria and sent in troops to put down violence between Maronites, a Christian group, and Druze, members of an offshoot religion of Islam. In 1861, the French forced the Ottomans to establish a new home state for the Maronites, which would eventually become the nation of Lebanon. The French were becoming increasingly influential in the region.

Many Syrians wanted to break free from both Ottoman rule and the growing influence of European countries. Arabs throughout the Middle East shared their desire to rid themselves of the Ottomans. In 1914, World War I (1914–1918) broke out in Europe. France, Great Britain, Russia, and eventually the United States—the Allied Powers—

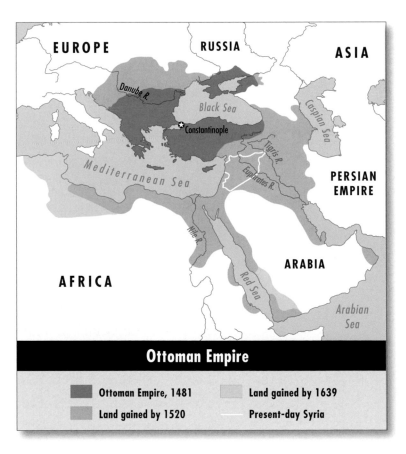

EUROPE   RUSSIA   ASIA

Danube R.

Black Sea

Constantinople

Mediterranean Sea

Tigris R.

Euphrates R.

Caspian Sea

PERSIAN EMPIRE

Nile R.

ARABIA

AFRICA

Red Sea

Arabian Sea

Ottoman Empire

■ Ottoman Empire, 1481   ■ Land gained by 1639
■ Land gained by 1520   — Present-day Syria

fought against Germany and Austria-Hungary, the Central Powers. The Ottomans joined forces with the Germans. The Arabs joined the Allied Powers. In 1916, Arab forces led by Prince Faisal ibn Hussein launched their first attacks against the Ottomans. In October 1918, the Arab forces, with assistance from the British, took control of Damascus.

Toward Independence

The war ended the following month with the defeat of Germany and the Ottoman Empire. Faisal was declared king of Syria, which at the time included Lebanon, Jordan, and Palestine. He declared Syria free and independent, and he began to prepare his nation for self-government. Syrian leaders started work on a new constitution.

France and Britain, however, wanted to maintain influence in the region, mainly to exploit its natural resources, particularly oil. They refused to recognize Syria's independence, and they divided the land. Syria and Lebanon went to France, and Palestine and Jordan went to Britain. With France now in control of Syria under what is known as the French Mandate, French became the language used in schools. The French also censored Syrian newspapers.

Having Europeans in control of Arab territory angered people throughout the region. Syrian nationalism grew, leading to several revolts against the French. During World War II (1939–1945), the French agreed to withdraw from Syria. On April 17, 1946, the last French troops left. At long last, Syria was a free and independent republic.

The Young Nation

The United Nations (UN), an international organization established to help prevent future wars, was founded at the end of World War II. In 1948, the UN divided British-controlled Palestine into two parts: an Arab state and a Jewish state, known as Israel. Many Arabs opposed the idea of a Jewish state being made in a land where the majority of the population was Arab and non-Jewish. Arab states in the region wanted to retake Palestine for its Arab inhabitatants. Only months after Israel was established, Syria, Jordan, and

In 1919, demonstrators gathered in Damascus to protest the French presence in Syria.

Egypt attacked Israel. Although Syria gained some land in the south, Israel won the war. Syrians blamed their leaders for the loss. The military forced Syrian president Shukri al-Quwatli out of office. This was the first of several military coups that rocked the young nation.

In the 1950s, Syria suffered from a series of ineffective governments and a poor economy. Syria turned to Egypt for assistance. The two nations combined to form a new state

In 1941, French general Georges Catroux (front left) read a statement declaring the end of the French Mandate in Syria. The last French troops did not leave until after the end of World War II.

Syrian troops push a gun into position during the war with Israel in 1948.

called the United Arab Republic (UAR). The union was unequal because Egypt had a larger population and a stronger economy. Additionally, the new nation was governed from Egypt, and many Egyptians secured powerful positions in Syrian territory. In 1961, Syrian army officers revolted and forced Syria to withdraw from the UAR.

During this time, the Baath Party began to gain strength in Syria. The Baathists wanted to introduce a socialist government to Syria to cure its economic ills. Under socialism, the government would control the economy by owning the means of production, such as factories and mines. The Baathists also favored Arab unity and freedom from foreign intervention. On March 8, 1963, the Baath Party, supported by army officers, took control of the government. Since then, the Baathists have ruled Syria.

In June 1967, Israel attacked Egypt, beginning what is called the Six-Day War or the June War. Syria fought with Egypt and Jordan against Israel. The Israelis defeated the Arabs once again, this time taking land from each defeated nation. Syria lost the Golan Heights, a hilly area in the southern part of the nation. The Golan Heights remains under Israeli control. The loss of the Golan Heights caused bitterness and division within Syria's political leadership, which gave rise to a new politician in Syria—Hafez al-Assad.

The al-Assad Regime

Hafez al-Assad, a Baath Party member and general in the Syrian air force, took advantage of the political upheaval. In October 1970, his troops helped him take control of the party, and the following year, he became president of Syria, a position he held for twenty-nine years. As president, al-Assad began land reform, taking the holdings of wealthy landowners and giving small plots to farmworkers. He improved Syria's education system and worked to develop the economy. Under his rule, however, Syrians had very limited freedom of speech and very few political rights. Many who spoke out against his regime were arrested, tortured, and executed by his brutal security forces. In 1982, these forces put down an uprising in the city of Hamah. Most of the more than ten thousand people massacred in this clash had not been involved in the uprising.

Al-Assad faced many problems with neighboring nations. In October 1973, Syria and Egypt attacked Israel. Early in the war, the Arabs pushed the Israelis out of the Golan Heights.

But by the second week of the war, the Israelis, with the help of an American airlift of supplies, had retaken the area.

Then, in the mid-1970s, Syria became involved in a civil war in Lebanon between Christians and Muslims. Al-Assad sent thousands of Syrian troops to assist a Christian faction that had asked for help. The Syrian army took control of parts of eastern and northern Lebanon. The Syrians remained in Lebanon for almost thirty years, before finally pulling out in 2005.

Throughout the 1990s and 2000s, Syria and Israel engaged in peace talks over the return of the occupied Golan Heights to Syria. Early negotiations were promising, but in the end little progress was made.

Hafez al-Assad ruled Syria for nearly thirty years.

Civil war has brought death and destruction to Syria. This street in the city of Homs was destroyed in the fighting.

Unrest and Civil War

Upon Hafez al-Assad's death in 2000, his son Bashar became president. Bashar al-Assad promised governmental reforms. Although many political prisoners were released, freedom of the press and freedom of speech remained limited. Social media sites such as YouTube and Facebook have been blocked.

In early 2011, a group of young teenagers in the southern city of Dar'a scrawled graffiti opposing al-Assad on a school wall. The teenagers were arrested and tortured. This ignited protests that became widespread. All across the country Syrian protesters began demanding political reforms and more individual freedoms. The protesters represented a cross section of Syrian society. They were young and old, Muslim and

Christian, rural and urban. Al-Assad's regime answered the protests with violence, and by fall 2011, many nations were demanding that al-Assad resign. Al-Assad refused, however, and blamed foreign nations for plotting and supporting the uprising in his nation.

For the first six months of the uprising, the protesters remained nonviolent. But by 2012, Syria was engulfed in a full-scale civil war. Tens of thousands of rebels, Syrian army and security forces, and innocent civilians were killed. Hundreds of thousands of Syrians fled into neighboring countries to escape the violence. Al-Assad's handling of the violent situation was severely criticized by nations around the world, including most Arab countries. As the upheaval continues, Syria's future remains uncertain.

Escaping Civil War

Hundreds of thousands of Syrian residents have fled into nearby countries to escape the increasing violence in their nation. In late 2012, an average of two to three thousand refugees fled the country each day. On a single day in November 2012, at least eleven thousand Syrians escaped into Turkey, Jordan, and Lebanon. Many of the men, women, and children—often wounded or injured—climbed over razor-sharp wire fences to seek safety in the neighboring countries. Many of the refugees who slipped into Turkey were taken to nearby refugee camps or to stay with Turkish relatives. The United Nations estimates that at least 408,000 refugees had left Syria by the end of 2012.

CHAPTER 5

A Powerful Government

THE SYRIAN CONSTITUTION OF 1973 ESTABLISHED the nation as a socialist state. The constitution states that legislative power lies with Syrian voters and that freedom of speech and equality are guaranteed. In practice, however, power has been concentrated in the hands of a few people, particularly the president. The government also controls the economy.

A new constitution adopted in 2012 states that Syria is no longer a socialist state. The government plans to focus on developing public and private businesses to strengthen the nation's economy and create jobs. The new constitution reinforces the concept of protecting freedoms, but it remains to be seen if these principles will be enforced.

Opposite: **Syrians attend a demonstration in support of President Bashar al-Assad.**

Wael al-Halqi became the prime minister of Syria in 2012. He is a doctor who had previously served as the minister of health.

Executive Branch

The government of Syria has three branches: executive, legislative, and judicial. The president is the chief executive and controls all three branches of government. The new constitution states that the president is limited to two seven-year terms. All presidential candidates must be Muslim and more than forty years old. Candidates are also required to have the support of at least thirty-five members of the Syrian parliament. People must be at least eighteen years old to vote in the presidential election.

Syria's president has very broad powers. The president appoints the prime minister, two vice presidents, all members of the Council of Ministers and their deputies, and all members of the Supreme Constitutional Court. He or she can also dismiss any of these officials. The president is commander in chief of the military and can declare a state of national emergency without approval from any other governing body. The president also has the power to dissolve, or break up, the People's Assembly, Syria's legislative body. In such a case, new legislative elections would be held within sixty days.

From Doctor to President

Bashar al-Assad was born in Damascus in 1965, the second son of Syrian president Hafez al-Assad. Because his older brother, Basil, was expected to become the next president, Bashar chose to study medicine. He attended Damascus University and then continued his medical studies in London, England. When Basil died in a car accident in 1994, however, Bashar became next in line to succeed his father. He returned to Syria to learn about the government and the military. Hafez al-Assad died in 2000, and Bashar took power.

Bashar promised to reform the corrupt government and transform his father's brutal regime by introducing democracy to Syria. But Syria's finances were in terrible shape when Bashar assumed power, and widespread government corruption made it difficult to change the nation's state-controlled economy. In 2011, antigovernment protests began, and the al-Assad regime responded violently. By 2012, a full-scale civil war raged in Syria, and any hopes of al-Assad being a reformer had been destroyed.

The Council of Ministers consists of the prime minister, his or her deputies, and the ministers. The council, with roughly thirty-five members, drafts laws, prepares the national budget, and creates plans for national development.

National Government of Syria

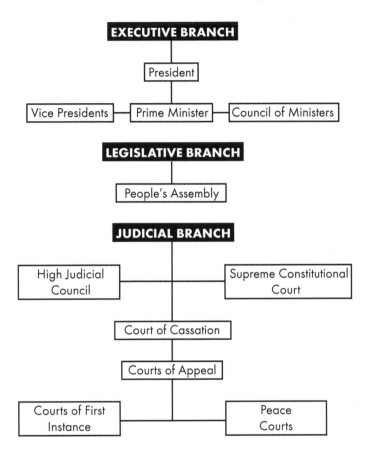

The Legislative Branch

The People's Assembly is Syria's legislative branch. It has 250 members who serve four-year terms. The assembly is made up of two main groups—the National Progressive Front (NPF) and the Popular Front for Change and Liberation—as well as independent members. Both fronts include several political parties. The assembly approves laws, treaties, and the budget. Half of the members of the People's Assembly must be workers and farmers.

The Judicial Branch

Syria's judicial system has many levels of courts. Although the 2012 constitution states that the "judicial authority is independent," in practice, the judicial system is under the president's control because he or she appoints and dismisses judges on all the courts.

The Supreme Constitutional Court is Syria's highest court. The court consists of the president and four judges. The Supreme Constitutional Court rules on disputed elections

A woman votes in an election in Damascus in 2011. Women gained the right to vote in Syria in 1949.

and the constitutionality of laws and regulations. The High Judicial Council, chaired by Syria's president, appoints and dismisses judges on all other courts.

The Court of Cassation is Syria's supreme court. Under it are courts of appeal that hear appeals on criminal or civil cases. Court cases are first tried in courts of first instance and peace courts. Religious courts deal with issues of Islamic, Christian, or Jewish law relating to children, marriage, and divorce.

Regional Government

Syria has fourteen districts, or regional governments, called *muhafazat*. Each district is named for its capital city, and a governor heads its government. The governor is appointed by Syria's Minister of the Interior and approved by the Council of Ministers. Governors report to the president. An elected council assists the governor.

The muhafazat are divided into a total of sixty-one districts called *manatiq*, which are divided again into subdistricts, or *nawahi*. The main job of regional and local administrations is to collect taxes.

الف مبروك

الف مبروك فرع جامعة دمشق للح

الف مبروك فرع جامعة دمشق للح

Baath supporters wave posters of Bashar al-Assad at a demonstration in Damascus.

Political Parties

The 1973 constitution stated that the "Arab Socialist Baath Party leads the state and society." The 2012 constitution no longer includes that statement, but the Baath Party still controls many aspects of Syrian society: the legislature and courts, the economy, the media, education, and the military.

In 1972, the Baath Party formed the National Progressive Front (NPF). The NPF is made up of the Baath Party and five smaller parties. In the 2012 elections, the NPF won 67 percent of the seats in the People's Assembly, independents won 30 percent, and the Popular Front won 3 percent.

The Military

The military plays an important role in Syrian life. Largely because of its long history of conflict with Israel and its occupation of Lebanon, Syria has one of the largest military forces in the Middle East. The country spends about 6 percent of its gross domestic product on defense. That figure is about twice as much as the average for countries around the world.

The Syrian military consists of army, navy, air force, air defense, and paramilitary forces. At age eighteen, all Syrian men must serve in the military for eighteen months. In addition to national defense, the armed forces are responsible for road construction, public works, and public health. Currently,

A Syrian jet races through the sky during a celebration of the 'Id al-Adha festival.

about 300,000 people serve in the combined armed forces, with an additional 314,000 reserves. Paramilitary forces number about 108,000.

All Syrian men must serve in the armed forces.

A Look at the Capital

Damascus, Syria's capital and second-largest city, is home to roughly 2,500,000 people. It is one of the oldest, continuously inhabited cities in the world. Experts believe the area may have been inhabited as early as 6300 BCE, and some evidence indicates people might have occupied the site as early as 9000 BCE. Since ancient times, control of the city constantly changed hands. Early invaders included Hittites, Egyptians, and Aramaeans. In later centuries, Assyrians, Babylonians, Persians, Greeks, and Romans seized the city. Still later, it was under the control of Byzantines, Seljuk Turks, Mongols, Mamluks, Ottomans, and the French.

These many influences are evident in Damascus today, and the city maintains a rich mix of ancient sites. The Old City features the spectacular Umayyad Mosque, which dates to the eighth century CE; the medieval Citadel; al-Hamidiyah Souq, a huge marketplace; and the Azm Palace, an Ottoman residence that now houses a museum. Christian sites in the Old City include

the Chapel of Ananias, the only church in Damascus that dates to the first century of Christianity. Elsewhere in the city, important sites include the National Museum, which displays artifacts covering six thousand years of Syrian life, and Martyrs' Square, a central square that has been the site of many political demonstrations.

Other parts of Damascus are modern. It is estimated that the population of Damascus increased tenfold in the second half of the twentieth century, as people from rural areas moved into the city. Many areas that were once gardens and farms became residential areas.

The city is home to a range of industries, including textile manufacturing, food processing, and chemical industries. The city also has a thriving artistic scene and is a center of book publishing in Syria.

Damascus has a hot, dry climate. In summer, the temperature often tops 100°F (38°C). Winters are mild, with some rainfall and occasional snow. Annual rainfall is about 8 inches (20 cm).

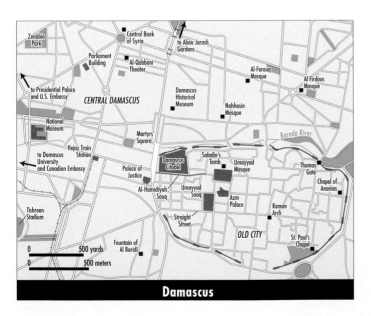

Damascus

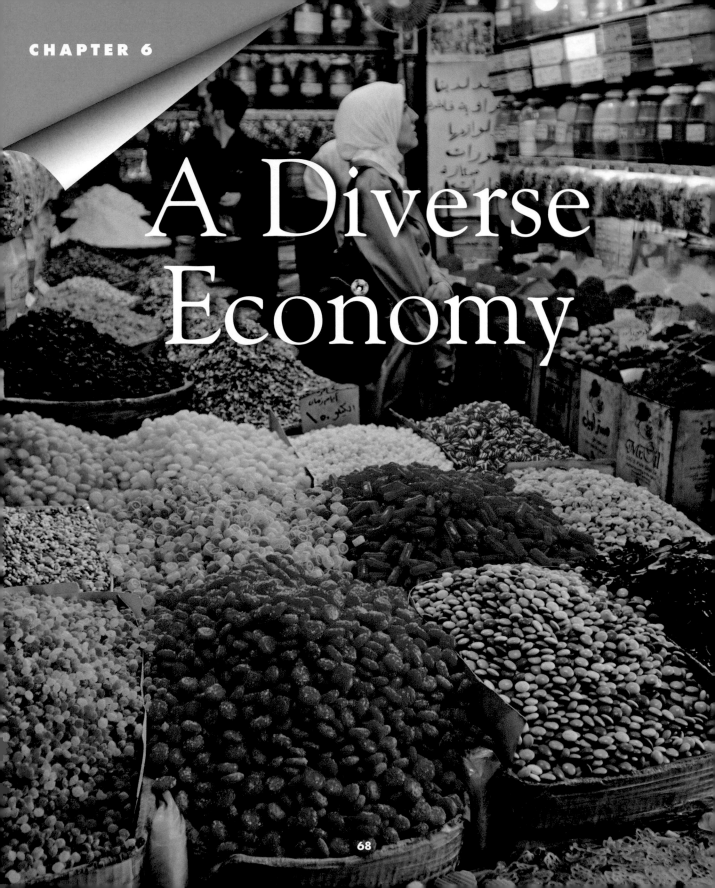

CHAPTER 6

A Diverse Economy

IN SYRIA, THE GOVERNMENT MAINTAINS CONTROL of the most important parts of the economy. It regulates private businesses. The government also operates the railways, oil refineries, electricity plants, and many manufacturing businesses. Syria has suffered significant economic setbacks as a result of the political unrest that began in 2011. The unrest has reduced the amount of goods and services the nation produces.

Syrians live in difficult times. About 35 percent live in poverty, and the population is growing quickly. The economy is not growing quickly enough to create the number of jobs needed to match the population growth. Unemployment is high in all age groups. It is particularly a problem among the young. It is estimated that about 70 percent of Syria's workers earn less than US$100 per month.

Opposite: **Goods are piled high at a candy and spice shop in Damascus.**

A man sells fresh lemons at a market in Damascus. Lemons are one of the nation's leading fruit products.

Agriculture

Agriculture is an important part of Syria's economy. It makes up about 21 percent of the nation's gross domestic product, the total value of goods and services a country produces in one year. About 17 percent of Syrian workers are employed in agriculture. Most land is privately owned.

Syria's agriculture sector has been successful because of the government's investment in huge irrigation systems. Dams on the Euphrates and Orontes Rivers provide much of the water for this irrigation. Production could be increased with additional irrigation, but high costs and recent dry spells have slowed down the expansion of farmable lands.

Syria's most valuable crops are wheat, barley, cotton, and sugar beets. Grapes are grown on the coastal plain and in northwestern Syria. Citrus fruits—oranges, lemons, and limes—are grown in abundance in the northeast, along with apples, apricots, peaches, and cherries. Other important crops include grapes, figs, melons, and pistachio nuts, which are grown mainly in the Aleppo area. Pistachios are so associated with Aleppo that in Arabic they are called *fustuq halabi*, which means "Aleppo nut."

Livestock is important to Syrian agriculture. Chickens, goats, and sheep are the main livestock animals. Syria also produces large quantities of eggs and milk products.

Mining

Oil is Syria's most important mineral resource. Oil was discovered in northeast Syria in 1956, and it quickly became central to the Syrian economy. Most of Syria's reserves of crude oil

Weights and Measures

Syria's official system of weights and measures is the metric system. In this system, the basic unit of length is the meter: 1 meter is equal to 39.4 inches, or 3.3 feet. The basic unit of weight is the kilogram: 1 kilogram, or kilo, is equal to 2.2 pounds.

A man tends a flock of sheep in northwestern Syria. In 2009, there were 21.7 million sheep in the nation.

Money Facts

Syria's official unit of currency is the Syrian pound (SYP). Coins come in denominations of 1, 2, 5, 10, and 25 pounds. Syrian bills, or banknotes, are issued with values of 50, 100, 200, 500, and 1,000 pounds. In 2013, US$1 equaled 71 Syrian pounds.

The banknotes feature colorful depictions of Syrian history, architecture, culture, and economy. The 50-pound note shows cuneiform writing on clay tablets from the city of Ebla, a picture of al-Assad National Library in Damascus, and a statue of former president Hafez al-Assad. The 100-pound note depicts an ancient stone gate and amphitheater in Bosra and the dome in the Umayyad Mosque.

are in the eastern part of the country near its border with Iraq. After years of diminishing production, new oil fields have been tapped, so there is hope that output will increase.

Syria also has large reserves of natural gas. Natural gas is often used in place of oil to run power stations, freeing up more Syrian oil for export.

Phosphate rock is another important part of Syria's mining industry. Phosphates are used to make fertilizers, most of which are exported to Europe. Most of Syria's phosphate mines are located near Palmyra.

Other mined resources include limestone, gypsum, sandstone, and asphalt, which are mainly used in building and road construction. The mountains hold small deposits of gold, lead, and iron ore, but not enough for large-scale mining projects.

Manufacturing and Energy

About 14 percent of Syria's economy is based upon manufacturing. The textile industry is one of Syria's most important manufacturing areas. Factories in Hamah, Damascus, Aleppo, and Homs spin locally grown cotton into thread and manufacture fabrics. Other major manufacturing industries include food, beverages, steel, chemicals, and car assembly.

Syria's primary sources of energy are thermal and hydroelectric power. Thermal power provides the nation with about two-thirds of the country's electricity. It is generated by thermal power stations that run on oil or natural gas. Hydroelectric power provides the other one-third of the nation's electricity. The Euphrates River plant generates most of the nation's hydroelectric power. Smaller stations on the Orontes and Barada Rivers also produce hydroelectric power, although in small quantities.

A Syrian works at a denim manufacturing plant. Textiles are among the nation's major industries.

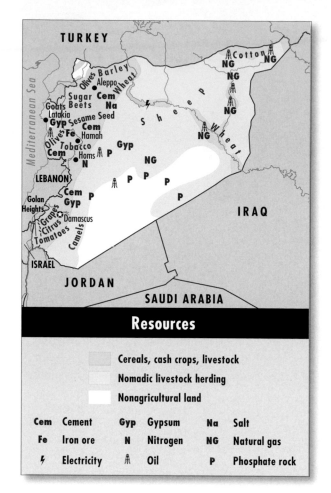

Resources

- Cereals, cash crops, livestock
- Nomadic livestock herding
- Nonagricultural land

Cem	Cement	Gyp	Gypsum	Na	Salt
Fe	Iron ore	N	Nitrogen	NG	Natural gas
⚡	Electricity	⚒	Oil	P	Phosphate rock

Tourism

Syria's wealth of historic sites, landmark buildings, and archaeological digs make it appealing to tourists. Six sites in Syria are listed as United Nations Educational, Scientific and Cultural Organization (UNESCO) World Heritage sites. They are Damascus, Bosra, Palmyra, Aleppo, the Krak des Chevaliers and Saladin castles, and the ancient villages of Northern Syria. UNESCO has identified these places as having special significance. Tragically, many of them have been damaged in the recent civil war.

Prior to the civil war, many millions of visitors came to these spots. Between 2008 and 2009, the number of tourists in Syria increased by 19 percent. European tourism to Syria surged by 54 percent during that period, and Arab tourists flocked to Syria in record numbers. In the first seven months of 2009, revenue from tourism topped US$2.7 billion. The future looked brighter than ever for Syria's tourist trade.

The political unrest that began in 2011, however, devastated the tourist industry. Revenue from tourism dropped 75 percent in the first eighteen months after the violence began. Two-thirds of the jobs in tourism have been lost. Many of the hotel rooms in Damascus that were once filled with tourists are now occupied by displaced families who have fled the violence around the capital.

Transportation

Syria has well-developed transportation networks that take people and goods around, into, and out of the nation. Very few people in Syria own cars. There are roughly 36 cars for every 1,000 people living there, compared to 627 cars per 1,000 people living in the United States. Most people travel by bus, by train, or on foot.

Most of Syria's major roads are located in the west. The country has a total of about 42,200 miles (68,000 km) of roads and highways, of which 38,000 miles (61,000 km) are paved. The major roads are the highways connecting Damascus and Aleppo and the road between Damascus and Baghdad, Iraq.

Tourists admire the view from the walls of the Krak des Chevaliers, a crusader castle in western Syria. In 2010, 8.5 million foreign tourists visited the country.

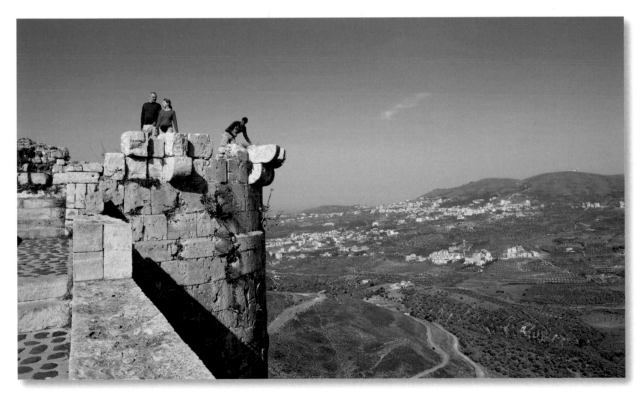

People board a train in Latakia. Railways connect Syria's major cities.

Syria's railway system includes about 1,329 miles (2,139 km) of track, most of it in the west. A major route connecting north to south runs from the Turkish border through Aleppo, Hamah, and Homs to Damascus. Another route out of Aleppo

What Is the Price in Syria?

Meal at an inexpensive restaurant:	366 SYP	($5.15)
1 liter (0.26 gallons) of milk:	70 SYP	($0.99)
1 loaf of white bread:	35 SYP	($0.49)
1 dozen eggs:	103 SYP	($1.45)
1 head of lettuce:	33 SYP	($0.47)
1 pair of brand name jeans:	7,055 SYP	($99.00)
1 pair of men's leather shoes:	3,351 SYP	($47.00)
1 liter (0.26 gal) of gasoline:	62 SYP	($0.87)

What Syria Grows, Makes, and Mines

AGRICULTURE (2009)

Wheat	3,701,784 metric tons
Tomatoes	1,165,611 metric tons
Olives	885,952 metric tons

MANUFACTURING (2007, VALUE ADDED)

Textiles	35,953,000,000 SYP
Food and beverages	28,975,000,000 SYP
Metals	20,003,000,000 SYP

MINING (2009)

Oil	146,146,000 barrels
Natural gas	6,040,000,000 cubic meters
Phosphate rock	2,466,000 metric tons

runs west through Idlib to the coastal cities of Latakia and Tartus before veering inland to Homs.

Both of Syria's main ports, Latakia and Tartus, were built after the nation achieved independence. Latakia is the main port for large containerships. Tartus hosts the only Russian naval base in the Mediterranean.

Syria's major airports are in Damascus, Aleppo, and Latakia. Syrian Arab Airlines, or Syrian Air, is the national airline. It operates international service to destinations in Europe, Asia, and North Africa, with its base of operations at the Damascus International Airport.

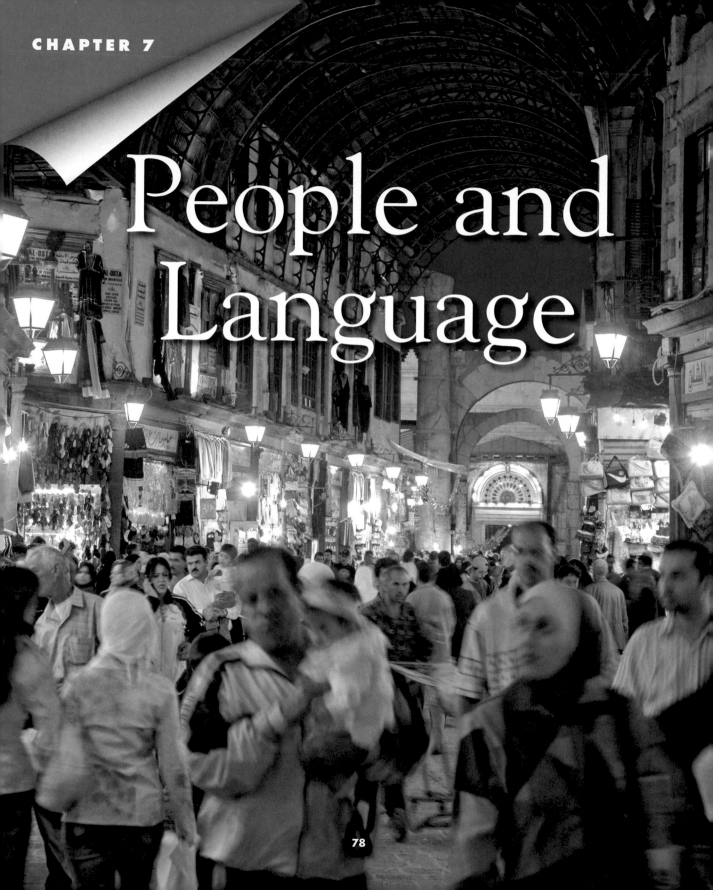

CHAPTER 7

People and Language

MANY DIFFERENT GROUPS OF PEOPLE HAVE inhabited Syria over thousands of years. These groups mingled to become the Syrian people. Most Syrians are Arabs, people who speak the Arabic language.

Opposite: **Shoppers stroll through al-Hamidiyah Souq, one of the busiest places in Damascus.**

In 2012, Syria had an estimated population of 22,530,746 people. That's a bit less than the number of people who live in the U.S. state of Texas. Syria averages about 314 people per square mile (122 per sq km), compared to 1,090 people per square mile (421 per sq km) in neighboring Lebanon or 89 per square mile (34 per sq km) in the United States. About 60 percent of Syrians live in cities, mostly in the west. More people move from the countryside to the cities each year. Many also live along the Euphrates River in the northwestern part of the country.

Syria has a young population. Thirty-five percent of its people are less than fifteen years old. In the United States, only 20 percent of the population is under fifteen. The average life expectancy for Syrians is seventy-five years.

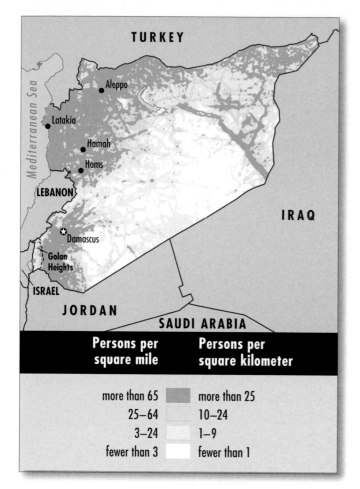

Persons per square mile / Persons per square kilometer

more than 65 / more than 25
25–64 / 10–24
3–24 / 1–9
fewer than 3 / fewer than 1

Population of Major Cities (2010 est.)	
Aleppo	2,900,000
Damascus	2,500,000
Homs	1,300,000
Latakia	991,000
Hamah	854,000

Diverse People

About 90 percent of Syrians are Arabs, people whose native language is Arabic. There are Muslim, Christian, and Jewish Arabs. Arabs and the Arabic language originated in the Arabian Peninsula south of Syria. Arabs migrated into the wider Middle East region long before the spread of Islam, though it was the Muslim conquests that began in the seventh century that made Arabs central to Middle Eastern history. The earliest Arabs were nomads called Bedouin. Today, most Syrian Arabs live in cities or are farmers, but Bedouin still live in the arid regions of eastern Syria.

The second-largest ethnic group in Syria is the Kurds, who make up about 9 percent of the total population. Kurdish settlements in Syria date back to the eleventh century. Kurds live mainly in the northeast and in large cities around the country. Millions of Kurds also live in nearby parts of Turkey, Iran, and Iraq. Many hope to carve out their own nation one day. Kurds speak their own language, Kurdish, although most Kurds also communicate well in Arabic. Most Kurds are Sunni Muslims. The Syrian government has long discriminated against Kurds. Kurds are not allowed to build Kurdish private schools or publish books written in Kurdish. Because of such restrictions, many Syrian Kurds have antigovernment feelings. In 2012, armed Kurdish rebels battled government forces and took control of several northern Kurdish-populated cities. The Kurds also fought other antigovernment forces, which had moved troops into Kurdish areas.

Other ethnic minorities living in Syria include Armenians, Turkmen, and Circassians. The first wave of Armenians arrived in Syria from lands to the north more than 2,500 years ago.

Who Lives in Syria?

Arabs	90%
Kurds	9%
Armenians, Turkmen, and others	1%

Kurds take part in a festival near Damascus. Roughly two million Kurds live in Syria.

Young Armenians work at a metal shop in Aleppo. The city has the largest Armenian population in Syria.

From Syria to America

Many American towns have been named after places in Syria. There are towns called Damascus in Arkansas, California, Georgia, Maryland, Ohio, Oregon, and Virginia. Thirteen states have towns named Palmyra. There is a Bozrah in Connecticut and a Hermon in New York.

A more recent wave of Armenians arrived as refugees fleeing Turkey during and after World War I. Most Armenians live in Aleppo. Another large group lives in the Quarter of the Armenians in Damascus. Armenians are Christians. They belong to the Armenian Orthodox Church or the Armenian Catholic Church. They speak their own language. Many Armenians work as small business owners, traders, or craftspeople.

The Turkmen came from central Asia. Most are Sunni Muslims and speak Arabic, although some speak Turkish. Some Turkmen herd livestock in northeastern Syria and along the southern Euphrates River. Others farm plots of land around Aleppo.

The Circassians are Sunni Muslims who came from southern Russia in the early and mid-nineteenth century to escape warfare. Most of them settled in the Golan Heights, although many fled after Israel captured that land in the Six-Day War of 1967. Some Circassians returned to the Golan Heights after hostilities ended. Today, a large population of Circassians lives in the Syrian-controlled town of Bir Ajam in the Golan Heights. Syrian Circassians speak Arabic, although some still speak their original Adyghe language. Many of Syria's Circassian people wish to return to Russia to escape the violence between the Bashar al-Assad regime and rebel forces.

Circassian dancers in traditional dress perform in Damascus.

Common Arabic Words and Phrases

al salaam alaykum	hello
sabah al-khayr	good morning
masaa al-khayr	good evening
shukran	thank you
ma' al-salama	good-bye
hal tatakallam al-'arabiya?	Do you speak Arabic?
hal tatakallam al-inkliiziya?	Do you speak English?

Languages

Nearly all Syrians speak Arabic, even if they also speak the language of their own ethnic group. There are many dialects, or versions, of Arabic used in Syria. The Qur'an, the holy book of Islam, is written in a version of Arabic called Classical

A sign in both Arabic and English points visitors to a museum in Palmyra.

Arabic. Modern Standard Arabic is used in Syria's schools, in printed materials, and on television and radio. Different dialects are also used in different parts of the country. They are sometimes so different that a Syrian living in Damascus may have difficulty communicating with a Syrian living only a few hundred miles away.

Arabic has its own alphabet, which includes twenty-eight letters. There are no capitals. Arabic is written and read from right to left.

Kurdish, Armenian, and Turkish are the other most common languages spoken in Syria. The most widely spoken foreign languages are French and English. Because of French influences in the twentieth century, many educated people in large cities speak French as well as Arabic. Children learn English in their early school years. In rural areas and villages, most people speak only their own Arabic dialect.

Education

The political unrest that began in 2011 has disrupted the education of many young Syrians. By 2013, the fighting had damaged 2,400 schools, and another 1,500 were being used as shelters. Even in places where schools remained open, many children did not attend school because of the violence.

Until the civil war, Syrians were proud of their education system, which had improved greatly in recent years. Public education in Syria is free from early primary school through college. Syrian law requires that children attend school from grades 1 through 9.

The Arabic Alphabet			
a	ا	d*	ض
b	ب	t*	ط
t	ت	z*	ظ
th	ث	a pause	ع
g	ج	gh	غ
h	ح	f	ف
kh	خ	q	ق
d	د	k	ك
dh	ذ	l	ل
r	ر	m	م
z	ز	n	ن
s	س	h	ه
sh	ش	w	و
s*	ص	y	ي

*Harder sounds

The education system is separated into three levels: basic education (grades 1 to 9), secondary education (grades 10 to 12), and university. Classes are taught in Arabic, although English is taught at the basic education level, and French is taught in grades 7 to 12. Final exams in the ninth grade determine if a student goes to an academic secondary school or to a technical secondary school. Technical secondary schools include industrial and agricultural schools for male students and crafts schools for female students. Commercial and computer science schools are available for both men and women. Final exams in academic secondary schools determine which college a student attends.

Syria's four public universities are in Damascus, Aleppo, Homs, and Latakia. Damascus also has the Syrian Virtual University, which provides a college education over the Internet to students all around the world. Private universities are located in Aleppo, Qamishli, Dayr 'Atiyah, Damascus, and Dayr al-Zawr.

Children on a field trip to Bosra. Some schoolchildren in Syria wear uniforms.

In recent years, girls began attending school in greater numbers. In 1999, for example, only 38 percent of girls attended secondary school. By 2010, that figure had jumped to 67 percent, matching the percentage of boys who attended secondary school. Equal percentages of men and women attend college.

College students relax in Damascus in the years before the civil war.

Speaking Without Words

There is a saying in Syria that "to tie the hands of a Syrian is to tie his tongue." Syrians frequently use gestures instead of speech. Sometimes they use gestures to emphasize what they are saying.

Syrians often say "thank you" by placing their right hand across their chest while nodding and gently closing their eyes. If this is done right after shaking someone's hand, this gesture shows a high degree of respect to the other person. Saying "no" can be communicated in several different ways. Quickly lifting the head while making a clicking sound with the tongue is one way. Raising one's eyebrows or jutting the chin forward also means "no."

Recent years have also seen a rise in literacy for Syrian women. The literacy rate for Syrian women of all ages is 77 percent, compared to 90 percent for men. In young people between the ages of fifteen and twenty-four, however, 93.6 percent of women are literate, compared to 96.1 percent of men.

An elderly Bedouin woman has a traditional tattoo on her face. Few young Bedouin today follow this practice.

Health

Hospitals and well-trained medical workers tend to be found in large cities, although public and private clinics have opened around the country. Health care in rural areas is generally poor. In public health care facilities, care is usually provided at no cost to the patient by the Syrian government.

Syrians are becoming increasingly healthy. In 2010, the percentage of infants and young children who die is half of what it was in 1990. A national program of vaccinations has eliminated or largely controlled diseases such as tuberculosis and diphtheria. In rural areas, however, particularly among the Bedouin, tuberculosis and trachoma, an eye disease, are widespread.

Women carry their babies while shopping in Aleppo. On average, Syrian women have just under three children.

CHAPTER 8

Religious Life

CENTURIES BEFORE ISLAM BECAME THE MOST common religion in Syria, many different civilizations had spread their own beliefs throughout the land. The Phoenicians, Babylonians, Assyrians, Greeks, Romans, and others each worshipped their many gods while in Syria. Their ancient practices were eventually replaced by the belief in one god— the monotheism of Judaism, Christianity, and Islam.

Syria does not have an official religion, and freedom of religion is guaranteed by Syria's constitution. Islam, however, is the predominant religion among Syrians. The president of Syria must be a follower of Islam, and Islamic laws provide the basis of Syria's laws and government policies.

Opposite: **Muslim women pray at the Umayyad Mosque in Damascus. When Muslims pray, they face in the direction of Mecca, Saudi Arabia, the holiest city in Islam.**

Islam

The religion of Islam traces its origins to the year 610 CE. Muslims believe that is when the angel Gabriel began speaking

A Syrian reads the Qur'an in a mosque. The word qur'an comes from an Arabic term meaning "the recitation" or "the act of reciting."

to the prophet Muhammad, giving him messages from Allah, the Arabic word for God. The messages instructed Muhammad to preach about Allah's holiness and power. The messages were collected into the Qur'an, the Muslim holy book. Allah is the same god worshipped by Christians and Jews. Islam has much in common with Christianity and Judaism. Muhammad accepted the Christian Bible as true, but he did not believe that Jesus Christ was the son of God. Instead, he believed that Jesus was a prophet. Islam accepts the teachings of many of the prophets in the Jewish Bible. Abraham, in particular, is an important figure in Islam.

Muhammad began spreading the word of Allah in Mecca, the city of his birth, and in nearby Medina. Both are located in what is now Saudi Arabia. It was not until after Muhammad's death, in 632, however, that his followers brought Islam to Syria.

Sunnis and Shi'is

Islam is divided into two major sects, or versions, Sunni and Shi'i. This division arose following the death of Muhammad. Different groups disagreed about who should be able to become caliph, the leader of all Muslims. The Sunnis thought that the caliph should be chosen from a group of elite Muslims. The Shi'is believed the caliph had to be a direct descendant of Muhammad.

The Shi'is do not recognize the authority of elected Muslim leaders. Shi'is believe their religious leaders have the divine right to lead because they were appointed by Muhammad or God himself. The Sunnis argue that the caliph should be elected. Religious power, they say, must be earned.

The Five Pillars of Islam

Muslims follow the Five Pillars of Islam, the most important rules found in the Qur'an. The first pillar, *shahadah*, requires believers to proclaim their belief by saying, "There is no God but God, and Muhammad is the messenger of God." *Salah* is the second pillar. It says that Muslims should pray five times a day: at dawn, noon, midafternoon, sunset, and night. The prayers can be recited in a mosque, at home, or outdoors. The third pillar, *zakat*, says that people should give charity to the needy. *Sawm*, or fasting, is the fourth pillar. This principle requires Muslims to not eat or drink from dawn to sunset each day during the holy month of Ramadan, the ninth month of the Islamic year. The final pillar is the *hajj*, a pilgrimage to Mecca, Islam's holiest city. If financially and physically possible, all Muslims must make this trip at least once during their lifetime.

In addition to this political difference, the two groups also have different religious practices. Sunnis, for example, believe that a Muslim can interact and communicate directly with God. Shi'is believe that communication with God must go through their religious leaders, called imams.

Around the world today, most Muslims are Sunni. The same is true in Syria, where about 74 percent of Muslims are Sunni, and 16 percent are Shi'i.

Other Sects

Syria's population also includes three smaller sects that derive from Islam: Ismaili, Alawite, and Druze. Ismailism is a version of Shi'i Islam. Roughly two hundred thousand Ismailis live in Syria today. Most live south of Salamiyah, between Homs and Aleppo, on land given to them by Abdulhamid II, a sultan of the Ottoman Empire.

About 2.6 million Alawis live in Syria, accounting for about 10 percent of the nation's population. They are Syria's largest religious minority. Most Alawis live in the Coastal Mountain Range along the Mediterranean, primarily around Latakia and Tartus. The Alawite religion is an offshoot of Shi'i Islam. Alawis take part in traditional Muslim practices, but most of the tenets, or beliefs, of their religion are kept secret by a group of elders.

Over the years, many Alawis joined Syria's military, and eventually they became the most powerful group in the armed forces. Some Alawis rose through the ranks to gain substantial influence in Syria. Their power further increased in 1971

Religion in Syria

Sunni Muslim	74%
Other Muslim (including Alawite and Druze)	16%
Christian	10%

Umayyad Mosque

The Umayyad Mosque of Damascus is one of the oldest and holiest mosques in the world. The site where the mosque stands has been sacred ground for different cultures for more than three thousand years. By 1000 BCE, Aramaeans had built a temple on that site for their god of storms and lightning. In the first century CE, the Romans built a large temple to Jupiter, their god of the sky, over the Aramaean temple. In the late fourth century, the Roman temple was destroyed and a Christian church was built in its place. The church was demolished and the present mosque was built between 706 and 715.

The mosque was originally covered with a wooden roof and supported by columns reused from Roman temples in the region. The courtyards and walkways were covered in colorful marble, gold, and glass tiles.

The mosque has been rebuilt several times after suffering damage from fires, invasions, and an earthquake. Today, the mosque remains one of the most impressive landmarks in the Islamic world, with a huge courtyard and prayer hall. Visitors marvel at the craftsmanship of the mosque's many original eighth-century mosaics (above). There are three minarets—tall spires with conical crowns—in the mosque complex. The tallest measures 253 feet (77 m) high.

Inside the mosque is a shrine said to contain the head of John the Baptist, who is honored as a prophet by both Muslims and Christians. The tomb of the sultan Saladin stands in a garden on the north side of the mosque.

when the Alawi general Hafez al-Assad became president. Since then, Syria has been under Alawi leadership.

The Druze live mainly in the southern area of Jabal al-Druze, a mountainous region in southwestern Syria. About five hundred thousand Druze live in Syria today. Their religion is also an offshoot of Shi'i Islam. The Druze are secretive about their practices. They do not pray in mosques and they do not admit new members to the religion. The Druze worship the Muslim leader al-Hakim bi-Amr Allah, who became caliph in 996. They believe he was an earthly incarnation of God.

An elderly Syrian Druze man. Syria has the world's largest Druze population, but Lebanon, Israel, and Venezuela have large populations also.

Christians and Jews

Most people in Syria were Christians or Jews before Islam arrived in the region. Today, Christians make up about 10 percent of Syria's population. Christianity in Syria developed from two different sources. One source was missionaries from the West who traveled to Syria to spread the teachings of Roman Catholicism and different Protestant religions. The second source, which accounts for most of Syria's Christian population today, was the Eastern Orthodox Church. The origin of this church dates back to the time of the Byzantine Empire.

St. Simeon's Church

St. Simeon Stylites the Elder (ca. 390–459 CE) became a passionate Christian at an early age. He believed that it was necessary to live a very simple life and deprive oneself of all comfort. This would help a person focus on faith.

Simeon, who was born in what is now Turkey, joined a monastery as a teenager. Later, after leaving the monastery, he shut himself up in a tiny hut, where he had little contact with other people. He further removed himself from others by living alone on the slopes of a nearby mountain. Crowds of pilgrims seeking his advice, however, interrupted his personal prayers. To escape their presence, he constructed a small platform

atop a pillar he discovered in ancient ruins in Aleppo. He lived on top of the platform for thirty-seven years, until his death. For nourishment, children from the village brought him food and goat's milk. In the fifth century CE, the Church of St. Simeon Stylites the Elder was built on the site to honor him. The pillar that Simeon lived atop still stands in the courtyard of the church.

Members of a Greek Orthodox church in Syria prepare for a baby's baptism.

Most Syrian Christians live in the west, near the coastal mountains. Their largest populations are near Damascus, Hamah, Latakia, and Aleppo. Most Syrian Christians are Arabs and share the same Arab cultural traditions as their Muslim neighbors. Many Christians in Syria are well educated and work in politics or in professions such as medicine and law.

A few Jews live in Damascus, Aleppo, and Qamishli. In 1948, two years after Syria became independent, thirty thousand Jews lived in Syria. Today, fewer than one hundred live there, and most of them are elderly. The tensions between Arabs and Jews that followed the establishment of the nation of Israel in 1948 forced many Jews to flee Syria. Those who remained faced discrimination. To this day, Jews are prohibited from holding governmental jobs. In 1992, President Hafez al-Assad allowed most Jews to leave Syria.

Holidays

Most celebrations in Syria are religious. The most important Muslim festivals are Ramadan, 'Id al-Fitr, and 'Id al-Adha. During Ramadan, the ninth month of the Islamic calendar, Muslims fast each day from sunrise until sunset. During this time, Muslims take time to reflect on spiritual matters. After sundown each day, people gather for an evening meal, or *iftar*. The table is spread with great quantities of food, and people enjoy fine treats and the warm company of family and friends.

'Id al-Fitr marks the end of Ramadan. The joyous holiday lasts for three days. 'Id al-Fitr is celebrated with special foods and tasty sweets, such as desserts filled with dates or nuts. During the day, Syrians visit their friends and relatives. People

A Syrian family enjoys a meal after sundown during Ramadan.

usually wear new clothing during the holiday, and children receive gifts of money from their relatives. Carnival rides and horse rides are set up in large parks for youngsters to enjoy. Also, fireworks are set off as part of the celebration.

'Id al-Adha, or the feast of the sacrifice, marks the end of the hajj. It is a time to remember the story of Abraham that appears in the Bible and the Qur'an. In the story, God commands Abraham to kill his young son in order to test the old man's faith. God sees that Abraham is willing to obey the command, so he has Abraham kill a lamb instead. 'Id al-Adha begins with morning prayers. After the prayers, Muslims slaughter a goat,

A shopkeeper prepares displays of delicious treats for the festival of 'Id al-Adha.

sheep, or cow. They give one-third of the meat to the poor and another third to family members. They keep the last third for themselves and prepare it for the family feast. Visits to family members fill up the day, during which Muslims ask each other for forgiveness for any wrongdoing they've done to one another.

Syrian Christians celebrate Christmas to mark the birth of Jesus Christ, whom they believe was the son of God. Families celebrate by lighting a bonfire in the yard and gathering around it to sing hymns. Few families put up decorations. Instead, people celebrate Christmas Eve and Christmas Day with family meals and church services. On Christmas Eve, Syrian Christians lock their gates. They do this to recall the times when Christians had to worship in secret because they would be persecuted for their religious beliefs. Easter is also an important holiday for Syrian Christians. The celebrations are highlighted by joyous family gatherings, religious services, and church parades.

A child selects an egg at an Easter service in Damascus.

CHAPTER 9

Rich
Traditions

SYRIA'S LONG HISTORY HAS GIVEN BIRTH TO A RICH and colorful cultural heritage. Astonishing sculptures and ceramics date back thousands of years. Syria's museums showcase collections of ancient bowls, jars, vases, and remainders of mosaic floors. Modern Syrian culture ranges from classic and modern poetry and literature to embroidery, metalwork, jewelry, glasswork, and the performing arts. Many of these artistic forms reflect Syria's prominence as a crossroads of trade, incorporating influences from Africa, Europe, and Asia.

Opposite: **Syria has a proud tradition of glassblowing. This bottle dates to the thirteenth century.**

Crafts

Through the centuries, Syria has been a worldwide center for crafts that are both useful and amazingly beautiful. Because some Muslims believe Islamic law forbids showing people or animals in artwork, many craftspeople use geometric shapes, hand lettering, or flowers in their creations.

Syrians have been making fine silk cloth for centuries.

Fabric makers in Syria produce stunning clothing, carpets, tablecloths, and pillowcases. Bedouin work on large, hand-made looms to create many carpets. Modern factories also produce large quantities of these items. Carpets are most often used as floor coverings or prayer rugs. Large carpets are also hung on walls as decoration. Syria's thriving clothing industry produces traditional garments that feature a wide variety of embroidery. Dresses, capes, jackets, and gowns are manufactured in bright colors and have rich, complex designs.

Silk damask, a fine cloth used to make sheets and tablecloths, was first made in Syria and is named for the capital, Damascus. Originally, damask was made from silk interwoven with silver and gold threads. Damask gained widespread popularity in the eleventh century when crusaders brought it back to Europe. Today, many other types of cloth are used in addition to silk. The unique weave used in damask creates a raised pattern on both sides of the cloth.

Syrian metalwork, made with gold, silver, brass, and copper, ranks among the world's finest. Syrian metalworkers produce handsome jewelry. Bedouin women often wear attractive chains and silver coin-shaped ornaments on their head coverings. Silver is also used to make trays, baskets, and eating utensils. Brass and copper craftspeople make attractive, durable plates, pitchers, and bowls. Until the mid-eighteenth century, Syria produced Damascus steel. It is extremely durable and was used to make swords. Damascus steel has a unique, wavy pattern that looks like flowing water.

Inlaid woodworking is another traditional Syrian craft. In a process called intarsia, craftspeople insert small pieces of bone

The National Museum of Aleppo

A visit to the National Museum of Aleppo offers a window into the rich archaeological history of Syria. The museum features a wide variety of artifacts, including statues, pottery, coins, glassware, tools, and examples of cuneiform writing. Most of the artifacts come from sites in the northern part of the country.

Visitors enter the museum by passing through a temple gateway that features a sphinx from the ninth century BCE. The sphinx comes from Tel Halaf, an ancient Hittite settlement on the Syria–Turkey border.

One of the museum's most important exhibits is the Hall of Arslan Tash, a thriving city conquered by the Assyrians in the ninth century BCE. The hall features handsomely carved ivory objects (left) of extraordinary quality. The gardens surrounding the museum are dotted with statues and stone objects from Greek, Roman, and Byzantine periods.

and mother-of-pearl, a material that lines the inside of oyster and mussel shells, into pieces of wood to create stunning designs. Items that feature intarsia include coffee tables and storage chests.

Handblown glass is another Syrian specialty. Vases, tea glasses, bowls, and other items are produced in rich colors.

Inlaid wood crafts are popular in Syria. Inlaid wood is used to decorate furniture, boxes, and many other items.

Literature

Syria's rich literary heritage dates back more than one thousand years. At that time, writers in Syria were at the forefront of the golden age of Arab literature. Abu al-Tayyib al-Mutanabbi (915–965) is considered one of the greatest poets in the Arabic language. Many of his poems praised kings he visited, and many described military battles of the time. His poems are still widely read in the Arab world.

Another writer and philosopher from the same period, Abu al-Ala al-Ma'arri (973–1057), rejected the idea that any religion contained special truths and considered the words of prophets to be lies. Al-Ma'arri called the hajj, the Muslim pilgrimage to Mecca, "a heathen's journey." His best-known works are *The Tinder Spark*, a collection of poems, and *The Epistle of Forgiveness*, in which al-Ma'arri describes a visit to heaven.

Poetry has continued to be important in Syria in more recent times. Nizar Qabbani (1923–1998) often wrote elegant, romantic poems. He also delved into social and political issues. Ali Ahmad Said (1930–), also known as Adonis, is one of Syria's most influential poets. Born in Latakia, he studied at the Syrian University in Damascus (now called Damascus University) and received a degree in philosophy. In the 1950s, he was imprisoned for his criticism of the social and political structure of Syria. After his release, Adonis founded two important literary magazines, *Shi'r* (Poetry) and *Mawaqif* (Perspectives). His work was revolutionary, breaking from traditional Arab forms of poetry to introduce unrhymed verses and prose into his poems.

Ali Ahmad Said, known as Adonis, has written more than twenty books of poetry and essays.

Ghada al-Samman (1942–) is one of Syria's most important fiction writers. Born in Damascus, al-Samman studied at Damascus University and the American University of Beirut in Lebanon. For a time, she worked as a radio producer and journalist for several Arab magazines. Her novels *Beirut Nightmares* and *The Eve of Billion* established her as one of the Arab world's most prominent writers. She writes about the uneasy social and economic conditions of the modern world and the isolation she sometimes feels being a woman writer.

Zakaria Tamer (1931–) writes short stories and children's stories that often deal with people's brutality toward others and the oppression of poor people by rich people. He has been an outspoken critic of the political regimes and social problems of Syria. Tamer had been prevented from publishing his stories in Syria by the Bashar al-Assad regime. After the outbreak of the 2011 uprising, he left Damascus and settled in Oxford, England. He is a strong supporter of the antigovernment movement.

Art

Until the nineteenth century, most art in Syria was created to decorate buildings, such as mosques and palaces. One of Syria's earliest painters to gain fame was Tawfiq Tarek (1875–1940). Tarek was born in Damascus and studied art and engineering in France. Upon his return to Syria, he supervised the restoration of several mosques in Damascus. His work includes portraits, landscapes, and historical events.

Mahmoud Hammad (1923–1988) studied art in Italy. He was the first Syrian artist to include Arabic letters in his artwork. Often the letterforms interact with geometric shapes to create abstract art. As a teacher at the College of Fine Arts at Damascus University, he influenced an entire new generation of Syrian artists.

Louai Kayyali (1934–1978) was one of the leaders of the Syrian modern art movement. His works include portraits, landscapes, and still lifes.

Many of the portraits by Louai Kayyali show sad or brooding people in everyday situations.

The Power of Cartoons

Ali Farzat is Syria's most famous political cartoonist. His drawings include no words. They often make fun of people in power. Farzat's work has appeared in newspapers and magazines around the world. In 2012, he was named one of the most influential people in the world by *Time* magazine.

Farzat was born in Hamah in 1951. His first professional work appeared when he was just fourteen years old in the pages of *Al-Ayyam*, a newspaper that was eventually banned by the ruling Baath Party. He later drew caricatures for two state-run daily papers. Farzat gained international fame in 1980 when he won first prize at a festival in Germany. His drawings then began appearing in the popular French newspaper *Le Monde*.

Farzat's illustrations are often critical of Arab regimes, especially those he believes to be corrupt and ineffective. Because of this, the governments of several Arab nations have banned his work. In 2000, he started his own periodical, *al-Domari*. This was the first independent publication in Syria since the Baath Party seized power in 1963. Despite the success of *al-Domari* and the international honors it earned, government censorship finally forced Farzat to shut down the publication.

Since the 2011 Syrian uprising, Farzat's work has become increasingly critical of the al-Assad regime. His support of the democratic movement in Syria, however, has made him a target. In August 2011, members of the Syrian security force grabbed Farzat from his car. They severely beat his hands and stole drawings he was carrying in his briefcase. Farzat was thrown on the road and later found by people who rushed him to a hospital. Despite the frightening experience, Farzat said he would continue to criticize al-Assad, saying, "I was born to be a cartoonist, to oppose, to have differences with regimes that do these bad things."

Music and Dance

Music and dance play an important role in Syrian life. Professional music and dance groups often enliven family gatherings. Musicians play traditional Middle Eastern instruments such as the *oud*, a lute, and the *rebab*, a fiddle. Drums and jingling percussion instruments often accompany the stringed instruments. Celebrations often include folk dances that date back centuries. The *debke* is one of Syria's most popular dances. In this line dance, the leader twirls a handkerchief or a string of beads. The dancers in the line join hands and keep the leader's rhythm while taking steps and kicking and stomping. Some ethnic groups maintain their cultural heritage through dance. The Kurds perform a dance called *govand*. In this dance, participants form a circle and hold hands, and then perform brisk dance steps while surrounding a pair of dancers in the center of the circle.

Modern music is also popular in Syria. George Wassouf (1961–) is one of the Middle East's most popular singers. He has more than thirty albums to his credit. Rouwaida Attieh (1982–) is known for her deep, powerful, expressive voice. She performs at many charity concerts.

A Bedouin man plays a rebab in Palmyra. Rebabs can have one, two, or three strings.

Film and Theater

Syrians often speak out about political issues in films and theater. Despite government restrictions on free speech, many actors, directors, and playwrights risk their safety to express their views. Duraid Lahham (1934–) is one of Syria's most famous actors. He has appeared in many movies focused on Syrian politics. In the 1970s, he earned fame for his

George Wassouf has been a popular performer since he was a teenager. He is nicknamed the Sultan of Music.

Duraid Lahham has been a popular actor since the 1960s.

portrayals of victims of the Hafez al-Assad regime. Yasser al-Azma (1942–) is a popular actor and writer of television, film, and stage productions. His work often pokes fun at Arab societies with their anti-American attitudes and beliefs. He has won many awards.

Abu Khalil al-Qabbani (1835–1902) was a playwright and composer who spoke out about government repression in the nineteenth century. Al-Qabbani is considered the father

Members of Syria's women's national soccer team practice their skills. The team has been taking part in international competitions since 2005.

of Syrian theater. One of his plays caused protests because it mocked a ninth-century caliph, Harun al-Rashid. The Ottoman government closed al-Qabbani's theater and banned performances of his works in Syria. Al-Qabbani left Syria and settled in Egypt, where he continued to produce his plays.

Saadallah Wannous (1941–1997) was a leading Arab playwright of recent times. His works, such as *The King Is the King*, are deeply political and look at politics and society with brutal honesty.

Sports

Soccer is the most widely played sport in Syria. Young children play the game at school and in the streets. The Premier League is Syria's professional soccer organization. The league includes fourteen teams. The top teams are Al-Wahda, Al-Karamah, Al-Jaish, and Al-Ittihad. Huge crowds attend soccer matches. Syria also has a national soccer team that is eligible to compete in the World Cup and the Summer Olympics.

Basketball is another popular sport in the country. There are both men's and women's leagues and a national team that represents Syria in international competitions.

Since Bashar al-Assad became president, he has encouraged sports as an activity for all Syrians. Under his administration, Syria has built or renovated many sports complexes and arenas. Weight lifting and martial arts such as karate and judo are popular in cities. Private health clubs and gyms are becoming common in Damascus. The government-funded General Union of Sports brings athletics into rural areas to encourage underprivileged children to get involved in sports.

Olympic Star

Ghada Shouaa is one of Syria's most accomplished athletes. At the 1996 Summer Olympics, she captured Syria's first and only Olympic gold medal by winning the women's heptathlon. The heptathlon is a series of seven athletic events that include two different runs, hurdles, the high jump, the long jump, the shot put, and the javelin. Before competing in track-and-field events, Shouaa played on the Syrian national basketball team. Her 1996 victory was only the third gold medal ever won by an Arab woman. Although injuries forced Shouaa to retire in 2000, she is still regarded as a national hero and inspiration to the Syrian people.

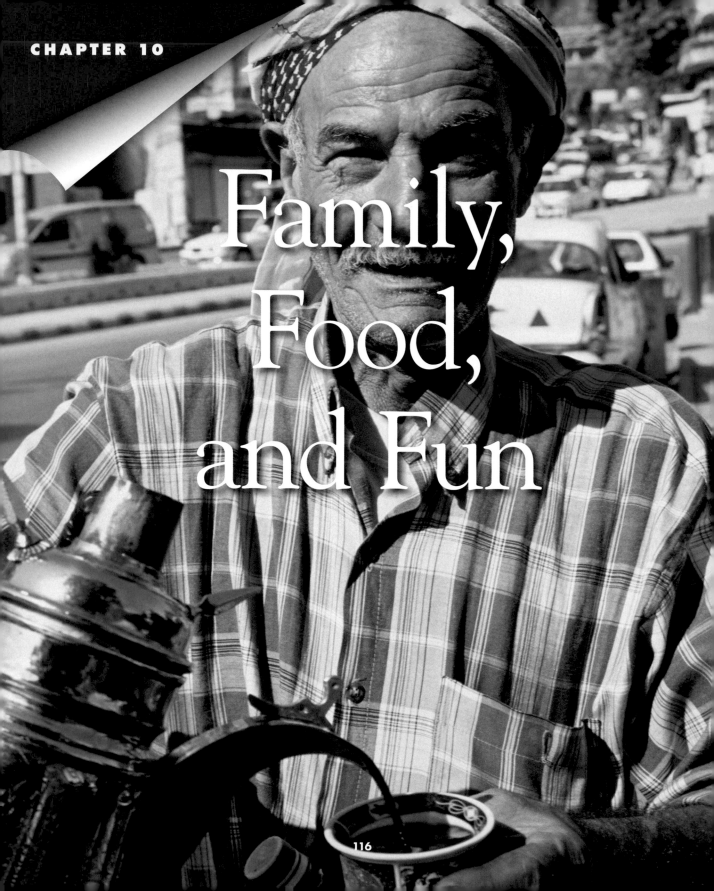

CHAPTER 10

Family, Food, and Fun

SOCIALIZING WITH FAMILY AND FRIENDS WHILE EATING fine foods, drinking tea, and talking about the events of the day are central to life in Syria. Syrians are warm, generous, and welcoming people who enjoy the company of their relatives and neighbors.

Food

Syrian food is a blend of many Middle Eastern cooking traditions. The result is food that is both delicious and nourishing. Some of the most commonly used ingredients are lamb, chicken, chickpeas, rice, eggplant, and bulgur, or cracked wheat. Fresh vegetables and fresh or dried fruit are also popular foods. Grapefruit, oranges, pears, figs, apricots, and plums are widely grown in Syria and can be enjoyed year-round.

Common dairy products include yogurt and goat's or sheep's milk. Olives are another favorite food, enjoyed in salads or as side dishes. Tasty spices, especially cinnamon, nutmeg, and clove, are also used in Syrian cooking.

Many dishes that have been eaten in Syria for centuries have become popular more recently in all parts of the world. Hummus is a dip that is made with sesame paste and chickpeas. Another dip called baba ghanouj is made with baked eggplant and sesame paste. Falafel, fried patties made with ground chickpeas, are now enjoyed throughout the world.

Meals

Falafel sandwiches are a popular snack in Syria.

Most Syrians eat three meals a day. Breakfast is usually eaten by 6:00 a.m. A typical Syrian breakfast might include olives, cheese, yogurt, and thick, sweet Turkish coffee for the adults.

Tasty Hummus

Hummus is a popular dip in Syria and many other places throughout the world. It is delicious, nutritious, and easy to prepare. Have an adult help you with this recipe.

Ingredients

1 16 oz. can of garbanzo beans

$\frac{1}{3}$ cup tahini (sesame paste)

$\frac{1}{4}$ cup lemon juice

$\frac{1}{2}$ teaspoon salt

2 cloves garlic, crushed

1 tablespoon olive oil

Directions

Place the garbanzo beans, tahini, lemon juice, salt, and garlic in a blender or food processor. Blend until smooth. Place the mixture in a serving bowl. Drizzle olive oil over the mixture. Serve with pita bread. Enjoy!

Syrian meals often include a number of small dishes.

Pita bread, served with a yogurt dip, melon, or sliced cucumber, is often set out on the breakfast table.

Lunch is typically the main meal of the day. It usually includes *mezze*, an assortment of appetizers that contains hummus, baba ghanouj, and tabbouleh, a salad made of tomatoes, onions, parsley, bulgur wheat, and mint. Mezze is usually served with bread and large leaves of lettuce. Main courses feature lamb, chicken, and, occasionally, seafood. *Kibbe*, a meat pie made with ground lamb mixed with bulgur wheat and pine nuts, is a favorite dinner dish. *Maqluba* is a hearty offering of lamb with eggplant, spices, and rice. Fish dishes are more commonly found in homes along the Mediterranean coast. There, families often enjoy dishes such as *sayyadieh*, a rich stew of fish and rice.

Dinner is similar to lunch, but lighter. Meals usually end with Turkish coffee or strong tea. For those with a sweet tooth, Syrian favorites include baklava and *kanafeh*. Baklava is a rich, sweet pastry made with layers of filo dough, chopped nuts, and syrup or honey. Kanafeh is a traditional dessert made with sweet white cheese, nuts, and syrup.

Syrians also enjoy snacking between their main meals. Small shops serve *shawarma*, thinly sliced lamb or chicken rolled up in pita bread. Falafel is another favorite snack food. In cities, street carts sell almonds dipped in salt, plums, corn on the cob, and roasted chestnuts. Juice shops serve fresh juices and beverages made with milk and fruit. Strawberry milk and banana milk are favorites.

A vendor sells snacks on the streets of Aleppo.

Housing

The kind of housing people have in Syria depends on where they live. In the cities, most people live in apartments. Some city dwellers own their apartments, while others rent. Families who own an apartment often have their parents and even grandparents living with them. A typical apartment is much like one in Western nations: it includes a kitchen, bedroom, bathroom, and living room, which can also serve as a dining room or additional sleeping space.

Most people in Damascus live in large apartment buildings.

Rural housing is mainly simple, single-family homes. In the western part of Syria, rural houses tend to be surrounded by olive trees and grapevines. Rural homes often have grape arbors over the roof to keep the blazing summer sun off the house. In the north, many people live in beehive-shaped houses made of mud brick, a material called adobe. These beehive houses protect their residents from extreme heat and cold. The thick bricks tend to keep the heat out, and the air that does become hot rises to the top of the beehive.

Some wealthy Syrians build large vacation homes in the mountains or near the Mediterranean coast. Many are extravagant and ornate. Huge chandeliers, brass floor lamps, and table lamps adorned with glass or images of flowers are often the focus of the furnishings in these homes. Air-conditioning is rare, so

Beehive houses in Syria date back at least to 3700 BCE.

Syrians rely on fans to cool their homes. The ceilings of these homes are high, which helps keep the rooms cool in the summer. Colorful cushions and pillows, many with dazzling geometric designs, provide seating. Many of these lavish homes are built around a courtyard with fountains, citrus trees, and flowers.

Women wearing long coats and veils cool off in the Mediterranean Sea at Latakia.

Clothing

Clothing in Syria is diverse, with people wearing a wide variety of garments. Many Syrians dress much like people do in

Syrian Weddings

Most Syrian couples today celebrate their wedding day much like people do in the West. The bride wears white, and everyone gathers for a party.

Some Syrians, however, maintain the traditional wedding customs that their grandparents observed. For the groom, the wedding day starts at 5:00 p.m., when his friends take him to the bathhouse, or *hammam*. After

bathing and celebrating with song, the men are greeted by an *'arada* band. The musicians in the band sing and act out sword fights during special celebrations. With cheerful song and beating drums, the band escorts the groom to his family where a night of religious chanting is already in progress. There, the groom's friends help dress him in his wedding suit, and the *'arada* band launches into flashy swordplay. Everyone accompanies the groom to the wedding site, where the bride is already celebrating with traditional wedding songs and belly dancing.

After the wedding ceremony, the guests enjoy a long night of eating and dancing. Typical food at a celebration includes meat, rice, and bulgur. In some places, everyone but the bride and groom dances together at the wedding. At these events, the bride and groom dance with their best friends, but not with each other.

Children play an important part in the wedding celebration, as they are allowed to playfully "steal" various items that the bride has brought along for the big day. After the wedding, the groom must pay the children to get back the items.

the West. They wear jeans and T-shirts, sweaters, jackets, and suits. According to the Qur'an, Muslims should dress modestly and not attract attention. Many Muslim women conform to this by covering their heads. Despite the hot climate, it is rare to see bare legs, upper arms, or shoulders.

Some Syrians dress more traditionally. For women, this might mean a *thob*, a long, dark dress with triangular sleeves that is made from heavy cotton. The dress is often embroidered around the neck, the chest, and the sides. Another type

National Holidays

New Year's Day	January 1
Orthodox Christmas	January 7
Revolution Day	March 8
Easter Sunday	March or April
Independence Day	April 17
Orthodox Easter Sunday	April or May
Labor Day	May 1
Martyrs' Day	May 6
Christmas Day	December 25

Many Muslim holidays are also public holidays. Their dates are determined according to the Islamic calendar. Because the Islamic calendar is about eleven days shorter than the Western calendar, Muslim holidays fall on different dates in the Western calendar each year. Here are some of those holidays:
Birth of Muhammad
Islamic New Year
'Id al-Fitr
'Id al-Adha

of dress has straight sleeves and is made of black sateen, a shiny cotton fabric. A caftan, a coat that buttons in the front, is often worn over a dress. Caftans usually reach to the ankles and have long, loose-fitting sleeves. Women might wrap a large silk cloth called a *shambar* over their heads.

For men, traditional clothing includes a long, loose-fitting shirt made of cotton. A *shirwal*, or cotton pants, is worn underneath the shirt. Men might wear a cloak, or *abaye*, that is made of lightweight silk or cotton. The abaye is open at the front and fastened with two cords. The neck and shoulders have colorful embroidery. Men sometimes wear a scarf, or *hatta*, on their heads. A head rope, or *agal*, holds it in place.

Celebrations

In addition to celebrating religious holidays, Syrians also enjoy nonreligious ones. For example, Revolution Day is celebrated on March 8. This holiday marks the anniversary of the March 1963 revolution when the Baath Party took power in Syria. Revolution Day is celebrated with large rallies where important government officials give speeches.

Independence Day is celebrated on April 17. On that day in 1946, the French occupation of Syria ended, and the Syrian Arab Republic was born. On Independence Day, Syrians proudly fly their national flag from their homes and along streets.

Although Syria is a young country, it has a long and vibrant history. Syrians remain proud of their past. And even as political unrest continues to shake their country, they look forward to a brighter future.

Many Syrians are young. About two-thirds of the population is under the age of thirty.

Timeline

<table>
<tr><td colspan="2">SYRIAN HISTORY</td><td colspan="2">WORLD HISTORY</td></tr>
<tr><td>Early settlements begin on the Euphrates River.</td><td>ca. 9000 BCE</td><td></td><td></td></tr>
<tr><td>Ebla is founded.</td><td>ca. 3500 BCE</td><td></td><td></td></tr>
<tr><td>Damascus, Aleppo, and Mari are founded.</td><td>3500 BCE–1800 BCE</td><td></td><td></td></tr>
<tr><td></td><td></td><td>ca. 2500 BCE</td><td>The Egyptians build the pyramids and the Sphinx in Giza.</td></tr>
<tr><td>Akkadians destroy Ebla.</td><td>ca. 2250 BCE</td><td></td><td></td></tr>
<tr><td>Phoenician civilization prospers in Syria.</td><td>ca. 1200–800 BCE</td><td></td><td></td></tr>
<tr><td>The Assyrians conquer Damascus.</td><td>732 BCE</td><td></td><td></td></tr>
<tr><td>Syria becomes a province of the Persian Empire.</td><td>539 BCE</td><td>ca. 563 BCE</td><td>The Buddha is born in India.</td></tr>
<tr><td>The Greek Seleucids take control of Syria.</td><td>332 BCE</td><td></td><td></td></tr>
<tr><td>The Romans conquer the Seleucids and take control of Syria.</td><td>64 BCE</td><td></td><td></td></tr>
<tr><td>Syria becomes part of the Byzantine Empire.</td><td>330 CE</td><td>313 CE</td><td>The Roman emperor Constantine legalizes Christianity.</td></tr>
<tr><td>Muslim forces conquer Syria.</td><td>636</td><td>610</td><td>The Prophet Muhammad begins preaching a new religion called Islam.</td></tr>
<tr><td>The Abbasid dynasty gains control of the region and moves the capital of the Muslim world from Damascus to Baghdad.</td><td>750</td><td></td><td></td></tr>
<tr><td></td><td></td><td>1054</td><td>The Eastern (Orthodox) and Western (Roman Catholic) Churches break apart.</td></tr>
<tr><td>Christian crusaders first enter Syria.</td><td>1098</td><td>1095</td><td>The Crusades begin.</td></tr>
<tr><td></td><td></td><td>1215</td><td>King John seals the Magna Carta.</td></tr>
<tr><td>The Mamluks of Egypt rule Syria.</td><td>1250–1400</td><td>1300s</td><td>The Renaissance begins in Italy.</td></tr>
<tr><td></td><td></td><td>1347</td><td>The plague sweeps through Europe.</td></tr>
<tr><td></td><td></td><td>1453</td><td>Ottoman Turks capture Constantinople, conquering the Byzantine Empire.</td></tr>
<tr><td></td><td></td><td>1492</td><td>Columbus arrives in North America.</td></tr>
</table>

SYRIAN HISTORY		WORLD HISTORY	
		1500s	Reformers break away from the Catholic Church, and Protestantism is born.
Syria becomes part of the Ottoman Empire.	**1516**		
		1776	The U.S. Declaration of Independence is signed.
		1789	The French Revolution begins.
		1865	The American Civil War ends.
		1879	The first practical lightbulb is invented.
		1914	World War I begins.
		1917	The Bolshevik Revolution brings communism to Russia.
Ottoman rule ends.	**1918**		
France officially takes control of Syria under the French Mandate.	**1923**	**1929**	A worldwide economic depression begins.
		1939	World War II begins.
		1945	World War II ends.
Syria becomes an independent nation.	**1946**		
Israel seizes control of the Golan Heights from Syria in the Six-Day War.	**1967**	**1969**	Humans land on the Moon.
Hafez al-Assad takes control of Syria in a military coup.	**1970**		
The Syrian army becomes involved in the Lebanese civil war.	**1976**	**1975**	The Vietnam War ends.
The Syrian army violently puts down a rebellion in Hamah, killing tens of thousands.	**1982**	**1989**	The Berlin Wall is torn down as communism crumbles in Eastern Europe.
		1991	The Soviet Union breaks into separate states.
Hafez al-Assad dies; his son, Bashar al-Assad, becomes president.	**2000**	**2001**	Terrorists attack the World Trade Center in New York City and the Pentagon near Washington, D.C.
		2004	A tsunami in the Indian Ocean destroys coastlines in Africa, India, and Southeast Asia.
		2008	The United States elects its first African American president.
Widespread demonstrations demanding political reform begin.	**2011**		
Political unrest turns into a civil war.	**2012**		

Fast Facts

Official name: Syrian Arab Republic

Capital: Damascus

Official language: Arabic

Damascus

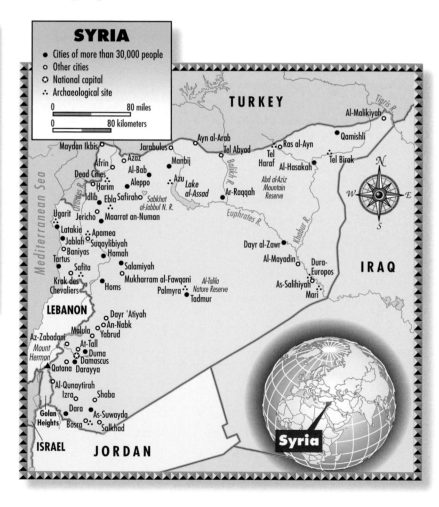

Syrian flag

Official religion:	None
Year of founding:	1946
National anthem:	"Humat al-Diyar" ("Defenders of the Homeland")
Government:	Republic under military regime
Head of state:	President
Head of government:	Prime minister
Total area:	71,498 square miles (185,180 sq km)
Bordering countries:	Turkey to the north, Iraq to the east and southeast, Jordan to the south, Israel and Lebanon to the west
Highest elevation:	Mount Hermon, 9,232 feet (2,814 m) above sea level
Lowest elevation:	Near Sea of Galilee, in an area occupied by Israel, 656 feet (200 m) below sea level
Longest river:	Euphrates River; 420 miles (680 km) flows through Syria
Largest lake:	Lake al-Jabbul, 60 square miles (155 sq km)
Average high temperature:	In Damascus, 55°F (13°C) in January, 98°F (37°C) in July; in Latakia, 60°F (16°C) in January, 84°F (29°C) in July
Average annual rainfall:	Coastal areas and western mountains: 29 to 39 inches (75 to 100 cm); inland: 4 to 10 inches (10 to 25 cm)

Mediterranean coast

Aleppo

Currency

National population (2012 est.): 22,530,746

Population of major cities (2010 est.):

Aleppo	2,900,000
Damascus	2,500,000
Homs	1,300,000
Latakia	991,000
Hamah	854,000

Landmarks:
- ▶ *Bosra Amphitheater*, Bosra
- ▶ *Citadel*, Aleppo
- ▶ *Ruins at Palmyra*
- ▶ *Umayyad Mosque*, Damascus
- ▶ *Waterwheels*, Hamah

Economy: The civil war has harmed many parts of the Syrian economy, most notably tourism and oil production. Agriculture is currently the most stable industry. Important crops include wheat, barley, cotton, olives, lentils, and fruits and vegetables. Syria's most important natural resources are oil, iron ore, gypsum, rock salt, phosphates, and hydropower. Textiles, food and beverages, steel, and chemicals are among the major manufactured goods.

Currency: The Syrian pound. In 2013, US$1 equaled 71 Syrian pounds.

System of weights and measures: Metric system

Literacy rate (2012): 84%

Children

Ghada Shouaa

Common Arabic words and phrases:

al salaam alaykum	hello
sabah al-khayr	good morning
masaa al-khayr	good evening
shukran	thank you
ma'al-salama	good-bye

Prominent Syrians:

Bashar al-Assad (1965–)
President

Hafez al-Assad (1930–2000)
President

Yasser al-Azma (1942–)
Writer and actor

Ali Farzat (1951–)
Political cartoonist

Abu Khalil al-Qabbani (1835–1902)
Playwright

Ghada Shouaa (1972–)
Olympic track-and-field athlete

Abu al-Tayyib al-Mutanabbi (915–965)
Poet

To Find Out More

Books

▶ Geyer, Flora. *Saladin: The Warrior Who Defended His People*. Washington, DC: National Geographic, 2006.

▶ Phillips, Douglas A. *Syria*. New York: Chelsea House, 2010.

▶ Zurlo, Tony. *Syria in the News: Past, Present, and Future*. Berkeley Heights, NJ: Enslow Publishers, 2006.

Music

▶ George Wassouf. *The Very Best of George Wassouf*. EMI Arabia, 2001.

▶ Jalal Joubi and Ensemble. *The Music of Syria*. Glendale CA: Hollywood Music, 2006.

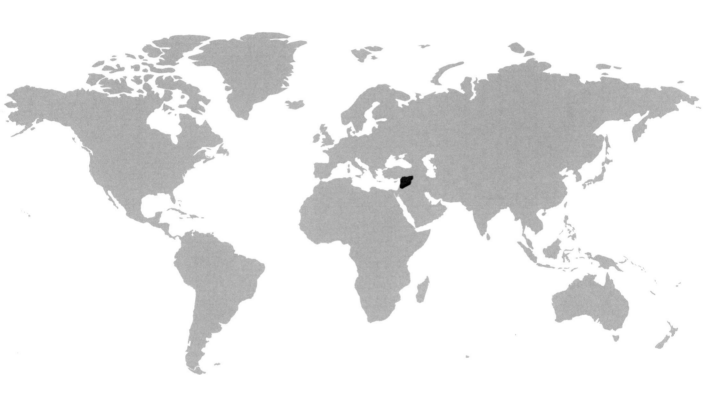

▶ Visit this Scholastic Web site for more information on Syria:
www.factsfornow.scholastic.com
Enter the keyword Syria

Index

Page numbers in *italics* indicate illustrations.

A

abaye (clothing), 126
Abbasid dynasty, 44
Abdulhamid II, 94
Abraham, 92, 100
Abu al-Ala al-Ma'arri, 107
Abu Rujmayn Mountains, 18
Adonis, 107, *108*
Adyghe language, 83
agriculture
    Aleppo, 71, 82
    coastal regions, 17
    crops, 17, 70–71, *70*, 77
    economy and, 70, 77
    education and, 86
    farmland, 32, 70
    fish farms, 30
    flooding and, 19
    government and, 70
    irrigation systems, 19, *19*, 22, *22*,
        25, 31, 40, 70
    livestock, 17, 19, 23, 32, 71, *71*,
        100–101, 117
    orchards, 17, 28, *28*
    People's Assembly and, 61
    rivers and, 21
    Roman Empire, 40
    steppe, 19, 32
    Turkmen and, 82
air-conditioning, 123–124

air pollution, 31, *32*
airports, 77
Akkadian people, *36*, 38, *38*
Alawis, 94, 96
Al-Ayyam newspaper, 110
Aleppo. *See also* cities.
    agriculture, 71, 82
    airports, 77
    Amorites and, 38
    Armenians in, 81, 82
    Christians in, 25, 98
    Church of St. Simeon Stylites the
        Elder, 97, *97*
    Citadel, 24, 25
    earthquakes, 24
    establishment of, 25, 37
    irrigation systems, *22*
    Ismailis in, 94
    Lake al-Assad and, *22*
    Mamluks and, 46
    manufacturing, 25, 73
    marketplaces, 89, *121*
    Mongols and, 46
    museums, 35, 105
    orchards, 28
    pollution, *32*
    population, 16, 25, 80
    railroads, 76–77
    roadways, 30, 75
    Sunni Muslims in, 25
    tourism, 25
    Turkish invasion of, 44
    Turkmen in, 82
    UNESCO sites, 74
    universities, 86
Alexander the Great, 40
Al-Hasakah, 16
Amorite people, 38
animal life
    bats, 29
    birds, 30, *31*, 33
    camels, 29–30

domesticated animals, 29–30
    gazelles, 33, *33*
    hunting, 29
    livestock, 17, 19, 23, 32, 71, *71*,
        100–101, 117
    mountains, 27
    steppe, 27, 29, 30
    Syrian brown bears, 29
    Syrian desert, 27, 29
    Syrian hamster, 30, *30*
    al-Talila Nature Reserve, 33
    al-Thawra Reserve, 33, *33*
Anti-Lebanon Mountains, 17, 23
Apamea, *40*
aqueducts, 40
Arabic language, 43, 79, 80, 82,
    83–85, *84*, *85*, 86
Arab Mountains, 18, 20
Arab people, 25, 43–44, 46, 48, 50, 52,
    53, 74, 79, 80, 81, 98, 107, 114, 115
'arada bands, 125
Aramaean people, 38, 95
Aramaic language, 39
Armenian Catholic Church, 82
Armenian language, 85
Armenian Orthodox Church, 82
Armenian people, 81–82, *82*
art, 35, 95, *95*, 103, 108–109, *109*,
    110, *110*
artifacts, *34*, 35, 36–37, 105, *105*
al-Assad, Bashar, 12, *12*, 13, 54, 55,
    56, 57, 59, *59*, 64, 108, 115, 133
al-Assad, Basil, 59
al-Assad, Hafez, 12, 52–53, *53*, 72, 96,
    98, 133
al-Assad National Library, 72
Assyrian people, 38–39
al-Atarib fort, 24
Attieh, Rouwaida, 111
Aurelian, emperor of Rome, 42
Austria-Hungary, 47, 48
Ayyubid dynasty, 45

al-Azma, Yasser, 113, 133
Azm Palace, 67

B

Baath Party, 12, 51–52, 64, 110, 127
Babylonians, 38, 39
Balikh River, 21
Barada River, 19, 23, 73
basketball, 115
Battle of Yarmuk, 43
Bedouin people, 21, 29–30, 80, 88, 89, 104, 105, *111*
beehive houses, 123, *123*
Bible (Christian holy book), 100
Bir Ajam, 82
Bishri Mountains, 18
borders, 15, 17
Bosra, 10, *41*, 72, 74, 86
Byzantine Empire, 10, 42, 43, 46, 96, 105

C

caftan (clothing), 126
calendar, 126
caliphs, 43, *44*, 93
camels, 29–30
capital city. *See* Damascus.
cars, *11*, 73, 75
Catroux, Georges, *50*
Chapel of Ananias, 67
children, 55, *55*, 63, 79, 86, 89, *89*, 115, *127*
Christianity, 10, 41, 43, 44–45, 47, 53, 67, 82, 92, 94, 96, 97, 98, *98*, 101, *101*
Christmas holiday, 101
Church of St. Simeon Stylites the Elder, 97, *97*
Circassians, 82
cities. *See also* Aleppo; Damascus; towns.
  air pollution, 31, *32*

Al-Hasakah, 16
Apamea, *40*
Bosra, 10, *41*, 72, 74, 86
Dayr al-Zawr, 86
Dayr 'Atiyah, 86
Ebla, 36–37, *36*, 72
Hamah, *19*, 22, 24, 25, 52, *73*, 77, 80, 98, *116*
Homs, 17, 22, 24, 25, *54*, 73, 76, 77, 80, 86
Idlib, 16
Latakia, *14*, 16, 25, *25*, 35, 76, 77, 80, 86, 98, *124*
Mari, 35, 37
Mecca, Saudi Arabia, 43, 90, 92, 93, *93*, 107
Palmyra, 8, 10, *20*, 39, *39*, 74, *111*
Qamishli, 86, 98
Tel Birak, 36
Tartus, 17, 76, 77
Ugarit, 37
civil war, 13, *13*, *54*, 55, 59, 74, 83, 87
Classical Arabic language, 84–85
climate, 16, 17, 18, 19, 20, 23–24, *24*, 28, 31, 67, 70, 125
clothing, *83*, 86, 100, 104, 124–126, *124*
Coastal Mountain Range, 17, 23, 27, 46
coastal plain, 15, 17
coastline, *14*, 15, 17, 25, 28, *124*
communications, 12, 48, 84–85, 107, 110
conservation, 28, 32–33
Constantine, emperor of Rome, 41, 42
Constantinople, 42
constitution, 48, 57, 58, 62, 64, 91
construction industry, 31, 72
cost of living, 76
Council of Ministers, 59, 60
Court of Cassation, 63
crafts, *102*, 103–106, *106*
Crusades, 10, 24, 45, *45*

cuneiform writing, *34*, 37, 72, 105
currency (Persian), 39
currency (Syrian pound), 72, *72*
Cyrus the Great, 39

D

Damascus. *See also* cities.
  airports, 11
  Barada River, 23
  Circassian dancers in, 83
  Citadel, 67
  Damascus International Airport, 77
  demonstrations in, 64, 67
  dialects in, 84
  earthquakes, 24
  elections in, *62*
  establishment of, 37
  al-Hamidiyah Souq, 78
  housing, 11, *122*
  invasions of, 38–39, 43, 44, 46, 67
  irrigation systems, 23
  map, 67
  Old City, 67
  orchards, 28
  Ottoman Turks and, 46
  population, 25, 46, 67, 80
  protests in, *13*, 49
  Quarter of the Armenians, 82
  railroads, 76
  roadways, *11*, 30, 75
  tourism, 74
  Turkish invasion and, 44
  Umayyad dynasty and, 43
  Umayyad Mosque, 67, *67*, 90, 95, *95*
  UNESCO sites, 74
  universities, 11, 86, 87, 107, 108, 109
  World War I and, 47–48
Damascus steel, 105
Damascus University, 59, 107
dams, 11, 22, 44, 70
dance, *83*, 111, 125, *125*

Dead Cities, 43, *43*
Dead Sea Fault System, 24
divorce, 63
Djade-al-Mughara site, 35
al-Domari magazine, 110
Druze Mountains. *See* Arab
  Mountains.
Druze Muslims, 18, 47, 96, *96*

E
earthquakes, 24, 95
Easter holiday, 101, *101*
Eastern Orthodox Church, 96
Eastern Roman Empire. *See* Byzantine
  Empire.
Ebla, 36–37, *36*, 72
economy
  agriculture and, 70, 77
  civil war and, 13
  conservation and, 33
  currency (Persian), 39
  currency (Syrian pound), 72, *72*
  government and, 57, 59, 60, 61,
    64, 69
  gross domestic product, 65, 70
  growth of, 69
  Hafez al-Assad and, 52
  jobs, 13, 57, 69, 70, 98
  manufacturing, 25, 67, 69, 73, *73*, 77
  military and, 65
  mining industry, 23, 71–72, 77
  oil industry, 17, 48, 69, 71–72
  pollution and, 31
  socialism and, 51
  taxes, 39, 63
  textile industry, 25, 67, 73, *73*, 104
  tourism, 23, 25, 74, *75*
  trade, 8, 25, 36, 37, 39, 40
education, 48, 80, 84–85, *85*–88, 86
Egypt, 50, 51, 52, 63, 114
elections, 58, 59, 62–63, *62*, 64
electricity, 11, 22, 69, 73

elevation, 16
English language, 84, 85, 86
Euphrates River, 9, 11, 16, *16*, 19, 21,
  22, 25, 28, 35, 38, 70, 73, 79, 82
executive branch of government, 12,
  12, 13, 52–53, *53*, 55, 57, 58–60,
  58, *59*, 61, 96

F
fabric-making, 104, *104*
Faisal, king of Syria, 48
families, 99, 101
Farzat, Ali, 110, *110*, 133
First Crusade, 45
Five Pillars of Islam, 93
flooding, 19
folk dances, 111
foods, 19, 30, 99, *99*, *100*, 101, *116*,
  117–118, *118*, 119, 120–121, *120*,
  121, 125
Fortress of Saladin, 26, 46, *46*, 74, 95
France, 47, 48–49, *49*, 50, 127
French language, 48, 85
French Mandate, 48, *50*

G
General Union of Sports, 115
geography
  borders, 15, 17
  coastal plain, 15, 17
  coastline, *14*, 15, 17, 25, 28, *124*
  desert, 8, 18, 20–21, *20*, *21*, 24,
    32, 33
  elevation, 16, 17
  lakes, 16, 22, *22*
  land area, 15, 16
  mountains, 16, *16*, 17–18, 20, 23, 26
  oases, 20, *20*, 21, 23, 39
  rivers, 9, 11, 16, *16*, 19, *19*, 21–23, 25
  steppe, 18–19, *18*, 27, 28, 29, 32, 33
  volcanoes, 18, 20
Germany, 48, 110

al-Ghutah Oasis, 23
Golan Heights, 15, 16, *16*, 18, 52, 53,
  82
government
  Baath Party, 12, 51–52, 64, 110, 127
  caliphs, 43, *44*, 93
  censorship and, 12, 13, 48, 52, 54,
    110
  Council of Ministers, 59, 60
  economy and, 57, 59, 60, 61, 64, 69
  High Judicial Council, 63
  laws, 60, 61, 91
  military coups, 12, 50
  National Progressive Front (NPF),
    61, 64
  People's Assembly, 59, 60, 64
  political parties, 12, 51–52, 61, 64,
    110, 127
  Popular Front for Change and
    Liberation, 61, 64
  protests against, 13, *13*, 49, 55, 57,
    59, 114
Great Britain, 47, 48
Greater Syria, 35, 40
Greek Empire, 10, 25, 39, 40, 105
gross domestic product, 65, 70

H
al-Hakim bi-Amr Allah, 96
Hall of Arslan Tash, 105
al-Halqi, Wael, 58
Hamah, *19*, 22, 24, 25, 52, 73, 77, 80,
  98, *116*
al-Hamidiyah Souq, 67
Hammad, Mahmoud, 109
hammam (bathhouse), 125
Hammurabi, king of Babylon, 38
Harun al-Rashid, 114
hatta (head scarf), 126
health care, 89
High Judicial Council, 63
historical maps. *See also* maps.

Ancient Syria, *37*
Crusades, *45*
Ottoman Empire, *47*
Hittite people, 38
holidays
    national, 126, 127
    religious, 65, 99–101, *100, 101,* 126
Homs, 17, 22, 24, 25, *54,* 73, 76, 77,
    80, 86
Homs Gap, 17, 45
housing, 11, 74, 122–124, *122, 123,* 127
"Humat al-Diyar" (national anthem), 66
hummus (food), 118, 119, *119*
hydroelectricity, 11, 22, 73

I

ibis birds, 33
'Id al-Adha holiday, 65, 100–101, *100*
'Id al-Fitr holiday, 99–100
Idlib, 16
imams, 94
independence, 11, *13,* 48, 50, 127
Independence Day, 127
infant mortality, 89
insect life, 33
Internet, 54
irrigation systems, 19, *19,* 22, *22,* 25,
    31, 40, 70. *See also* water.
Islamic religion. *See also* religion.
    Abraham and, 92
    al-Atarib fort, 24
    Alawis, 94, 96
    artwork and, 103
    calendar, 126
    caliphs, 43, *44*
    Circassians and, 82
    clothing and, 125
    Crusades and, 10, 45
    Druze Muslims, 18, 47, 96, *96*
    Five Pillars of Islam, 93
    government and, 58, 63, 91, 96
    'Id al-Adha holiday, 65, 100–101, *100*

'Id al-Fitr holiday, 99–100
imams, 94
Ismailism, 94
Jesus Christ and, 92
laws and, 91, 103
Mecca, Saudi Arabia, 43, 90, 92,
    93, *93,* 107
mosques, 10, 25, 67, *67,* 95, *95*
Muhammad, 43, 92, 93
national holidays and, 126
prayer, 90, 93, 100
Qur'an, 84, 92, *92,* 100, 125
Ramadan (Islamic holy month),
    93, 99, *99*
Shi'i Muslims, 93–94, 96
Sunni Muslims, 25, 80, 82, 93–94
Turkmen and, 82
Umayyad Mosque, 90, 95, *95*
Israel, 15, 16, 18, 49–50, *51,* 52–53,
    65, 98

J

Jabal al-Druze region, 96
Jerusalem, 45
Jesus Christ, 92, 101
jobs, 13, 57, 69, 70, 98
John the Baptist, 95
Jordan, 35, 48, 49, 52, 55
Judaism, 45, 49–50, 92, 98
judicial branch of government, 58, 59,
    61, 62–63
June War. *See* Six-Day War.

K

kanafeh (food), 121
Kayyali, Louai, 109, *109*
Khabur River, 21
Khalid ibn al-Walid, 25, 43
Krak des Chevaliers, 45, 74, *75*
Kurdish language, 80–81, 85
Kurdish people, 80, *81,* 111

L

Lahham, Duraid, 112–113, *113*
Lake al-Assad, 22, *22,* 33
Lake al-Jabbul, 16, 23
languages, *34,* 37, 39, 43, 48, 80, 81,
    82, 83, 84–85, *84, 85,* 86
Latakia, *14,* 16, 25, *25,* 35, 76, 77, 80,
    86, 98, *124*
laurel, 27
Lebanon, 35, 37, 42, 47, 48, 53, 55, 65
legislative branch of government, 58,
    59, *60,* 61
licorice, 27
life expectancy, 79
literacy rate, 88
literature, 107–108, *108*
lunch foods, 120

M

magazines, 107, 110
Mamluk dynasty, 45–46
manufacturing, 25, 67, 69, 73, *73,* 77
maps. *See also* historical maps.
    Damascus, 67
    geopolitical, *10*
    population density, 80
    resources, *71*
    topographical, *16*
maqluba (food), 120
Mardam Bey, Khalil, 66
Mari, 35, 37
marine life, 30, *31,* 120
marketplaces, 68, 70, 78
Maronite people, 47
marriage, 63, 125, *125*
martial arts, 115
Martyrs' Square, 67
Mecca, Saudi Arabia, 43, 90, 92, 93,
    93, 107
Mediterranean Sea, 9, *14,* 15, 17, 22,
    23, 25, 35, 94, *124*
Mesopotamia, 25, 36, 37, 38

metalwork, 105

metric system, 71

mezze (appetizers), 120

military, 11–12, *12*, 13, 50–51, *51*, 53, 55, 57, 65–66, *65*, 66

mining industry, 23, 71–72, 77

missionaries, 96

Mosque of Khalid ibn al-Walid, 25

mosques, 10, 25, 67, *67*, 95, *95*

Mount Hermon, 16, *16*, 17

movies, 112–113

Muawiyah I (caliph), 43, *44*

muhafazat (regional governments), 63

Muhammad (Muslim prophet), 43, 92, 93

music, 66, 111, *111*, *112*, 125

al-Mutanabbi, Abu al-Tayyib, 107, *133*

N

Naram-Sin, king of Akkad, 38, *38*

national airline, 77

national anthem, 66

National Environmental Action Plan (NEAP), 32–33

national flag, *13*, 63, *63*, 127

national holidays, 65, 126, 127

National Museum of Aleppo, 67, 105, *105*

National Progressive Front (NPF), 61, 64

national soccer team, 115

natural gas, 72

nawahi (subdistricts), 63

newspapers, 12, 48, 110

nomads. *See* Bedouin people.

norias (waterwheels), *19*, 25

O

oases, 20, *20*, 21, 23, 39

oil industry, 17, 48, 69, 71–72

Olympic Games, 115, *115*

orchards, 17, 28, *28*

Orontes River, 11, 19, *19*, 21, 22, 25, 28, 70, 73

Ottoman Empire, 46, 47–48, *47–48*, 94, 114

P

Palace of Ebla, *36*

Palmyra, 8, 10, *20*, 39, *39*, 74, *111*

Palmyrene Empire, 42, *42*

pelicans, *31*

people

    Arabs, 25, 43–44, 46, 48, 50, 52, 53, 74, 79, 80, 81, 98, 107, 114, 115

    Bedouin, 21, 29–30, 80, 88, 89, 104, 105, *111*

    early settlements, 35

    education, 48, 80, 84–85, *85–88*, 86

    ethnic groups, 80–82, 111

    families, 99, 101

    housing, 11, 74, 122–124, *122*, *123*, 127

    Maronites, 47

    military service, 65–66, 66

    population, 16, 25, 46, 67, 69, 79, 80

    women, 60, 62, 86, 87–88, *87*, *88*, 89, 108, *114*, 115, *115*, *124*, 125–126

People's Assembly, 59, 60, 64

Persian Empire, 39, 40

pets, 30, *30*

Phoenician people, 37, 46

phosphate mining, 72

plant life

    air pollution and, 31

    cities, 31

    coastline, 28

    commercial uses of, 27

    conservation, 28

    damask roses, 29, *29*

    date palm trees, *20*

    forests, 26, 27, 28

    mountains, 28

    oases, 20, *20*

    orchards, 17, 28, *28*

    reforestation projects, 28

    rural housing and, 123

    scrub underbrush, 28

    steppe, 28, 33

    Syrian Desert, 20, *20*, 24, 27, 33

    al-Thawra Reserve, 33

    wildflowers, 28

poetry, 107

political parties, 12, 51–52, 61, 64, 110, 127

pollution, 31

Pompey (Roman general), 40

Popular Front for Change and Liberation, 61, 64

population, 16, 25, 46, 67, 69, 79, 80

poverty, 69

prayers, 90, 93, 100

Premier League soccer organization, 114–115

presidents, 12, *12*, 13, 52–53, *53*, 54–55, 57, 58, 59, *59*, 96

prime ministers, 58, *58*, 59, 60

Protestantism, 96

protests, 13, *13*, 49, 55, 57, 59, 114

publishing industry, 67

Q

al-Qabbani, Abu Khalil, 113–114, *133*

Qabbani, Nizar, 107

Qamishli, 86, 98

Quarter of the Armenians, 82

Qur'an (Islamic holy book), 84, 92, *92*, 100, 125

al-Quwatli, Shukri, 50

R

radio, 12, 83
railroads, 11, 17, 47, 69, 76–77
Ramadan (Islamic holy month), 93, 99, 99
rebab (musical instrument), 111, *111*
recipe (hummus), 119, *119*
refugees, 55, *55*, 82
regional governments, 63
religion. *See also* Islamic religion.
    Alawis, 94, 96
    Christianity, 10, 41, 43, 44–45, 47, 53, 67, 82, 92, 94, 95, 96, 97, 98, *98*, 101, *101*
    Church of St. Simeon Stylites the Elder, 97, *97*
    clothing and, 125
    government and, 91, 98
    holidays, 65, 99–101, *100*, *101*, 126
Revolution Day, 127
roadways, 11, *11*, 17, 30, 40, 65, 72, 75
Roman Catholicism, 96
Roman Empire, 10, 40–42, *41*, 43, 95, 105
Russia, 47

S

Said, Ali Ahmad. *See* Adonis.
Saladin castle. *See* Fortress of Saladin.
Saladin (sultan), 45, 46
salaries, 69
Salim Flayfel, Ahmad, 66
Salim Flayfel, Mohammad, 66
salt mining, 23
al-Samman, Ghada, 108
Sea of Galilee, 16
Seleucid dynasty, 40, *40*
Seleucus (Greek general), 40
shambar (head scarf), 126
Shi'i Muslims, 93–94, 96

shipping industry, 77
shirwal (clothing), 126
Shouaa, Ghada, 115, *115*, 133, *133*
silk damask, 104, *104*
Simeon Stylites the Elder (saint), 97, *97*
Six-Day War, 15, 52, 82–83
soccer, 114–115, *114*
socialism, 51, 57
sports, 25, 114–115, *114*, *115*
steppe, 18–19, *18*, 27, 28, 29, 32, 33
Sunni Muslims, 25, 80, 82, 93–94
Supreme Constitutional Court, 59, 62–63
Syrian Desert, 8, 18, 20–21, *20*, *21*, 24, 32, 33
Syrian pound (currency), 72, *72*
Syrian Virtual University, 86

T

Tamer, Zakaria, 108
Tarek, Tawfiq, 109
Tartus, 17, 76, 77
taxes, 39, 63
tea, *116*, 121
television, 12, 83, 113
Temple of Baal, 39
textile industry, 25, 67, 73, *73*, 104
theater, 113–114
thermal power, 73
Third Crusade, 45
thob (clothing), 125
Tigris River, 9, 25, 38
tourism, 23, 25, 74, 75
towns. *See also* cities.
    Bir Ajam, 83
    United States, 82
trade, 8, 25, 36, 37, 39, 40
transportation, 11, *11*, 17, 31, 75–77
Turkey, 15, 18, 21, 22, 35, 36, 38, 42, 44, 45, 55, 76, 80, 82, 97
Turkish language, 82, 85
Turkmen, 82

U

Ugarit, 37
Umayyad dynasty, 43–44
Umayyad Mosque, 67, *67*, 72, 90, 95, *95*
United Arab Republic (UAR), 51, 63
United Nations Educational, Scientific and Cultural Organization (UNESCO) World Heritage sites, 74
United Nations (UN), 49, 55
United States, 47, 82

V

vaccinations, 89
vice presidents, 58, 59
volcanoes, 18, 20

W

wall paintings, 35
Wannous, Saadallah, 114
Wassouf, George, 111, *112*
water, 30–31, 40, 44. *See also* irrigation systems.
waterwheels, 19, *19*, 25
weights and measures, 71
Western Roman Empire, 42
wildflowers, 28
wildlife. *See* animal life; insect life; marine life; plant life.
women, 60, 62, 86, 87–88, *87*, *88*, 89, 108, *114*, 115, *115*, *124*, 125–126
World Cup soccer tournament, 115
World War I, 47–48, 82
World War II, 49

Y

Yarmuk River, 19

Z

Zenobia, queen of Palmyrene Empire, 42, *42*

Meet the Author

NEL YOMTOV IS AN AWARD-WINNING AUTHOR AND editor with a passion for writing nonfiction books for young people. Bitten by the reading bug at an early age, he learned how books could be the doorway to the wonders of our world and its people. Writing gives him an opportunity to investigate the subjects he loves best and to share his discoveries with young readers. In recent years, he has written books about history and geography as well as graphic-novel adaptations of classic mythology, sports biographies, and science topics.

Yomtov was born in New York City. After graduating college, he worked at Marvel Comics, where he handled all phases of comic book production work. By the time he left seven years later, he was supervisor of the product development division of Marvel's licensing program. Yomtov has also written, edited, and colored hundreds of Marvel comic books.

He has served as editorial director of a children's nonfiction book publisher and also as publisher of the Hammond World Atlas book division. In between, he squeezed in a two-year stint as consultant to Major League Baseball, where he helped supervise an educational program for elementary and middle schools throughout the country.

He lives in the New York area with his wife, Nancy, a teacher and writer, and son, Jess, a sports journalist. He spends his leisure hours on the softball fields in New York City's Central Park and at neighborhood blues clubs playing harmonica with local bands.

Photo Credits